OH, I DO LIKE TO BE BESIDE THE SEA-SIDE

HORRIBLE GEOGRAPHY

CRACKING COASTS

ANITA GANERI ILLUSTRATED BY MIKE PHILLIPS

■SCHOLASTIC

Also available
Bloomin' Rainforests • Desperate Deserts •
Earth-Shattering Earthquakes • Monster Lakes • Odious Oceans •
Perishing Poles • Raging Rivers • Stormy Weather •
Violent Volcanoes • Wild Islands

Horrible Geography Handbooks
Planet in Peril
Vile Volcanoes
Wicked Weather
Wild Animals

Specials
Intrepid Explorers
Horrible Geography of the World

Scholastic Children's Books,
Euston House, 24 Eversholt Street,
London NW1 1DB, UK

A division of Scholastic Ltd
London ~ New York ~ Toronto ~ Sydney ~ Auckland
Mexico City ~ New Delhi ~ Hong Kong

First published in the UK by Scholastic Ltd, 2006
This edition published 2010

Text copyright © Anita Ganeri, 2006
Illustrations copyright © Mike Phillips, 2006, 2010

ISBN 978 1407 11080 6

Page layout services provided by Quadrum Solutions Ltd, Mumbai, India
Printed and bound in the UK by CPI Bookmarque, Croydon, Surrey

2 4 6 8 10 9 7 5 3 1

The right of Anita Ganeri and Mike Phillips to be identified as the author and illustrator of this work
respectively has been asserted by them in accordance with the Copyright, Designs and Patents Act,
1988.

This is a horribly good way to show that
learning about our world can be fun.
And seriously important."

Michael Palin

CONTENTS

INTRODUCTION

At last! A Horrible Geography book that starts off with some good news. School's out for summer and you're heading off on your holidays. Yep – you're setting off to spend two sun-sational weeks on the coast. Two weeks of doing nothing but lounging about on a baking-hot beach. Bliss. So grab yourself an ice cream and settle down in a comfy deck chair. It's time to forget all about mindless maps and tongue-twisting place names you can't even pronounce. Time to wave bye-bye to geography lessons and geography teachers... Or is it? Who's that shadowy figure shuffling shiftily along the shore? Yikes! It's only your terrible teacher. And it's not a pretty sight. But what on Earth is he doing there? Unbelievably, he's picked the same bit of seaside as you have for his horrible summer hols! How unlucky is that?!

That's the trouble with Horrible Geography teachers. Like the irritating specks of sand stuck to your beach towel, they end up getting everywhere. And they're horribly hard to shake off. You see, geography's all about finding out about the world around you. So geography teachers are always rushing off to fascinating far-flung places (OK, in your case, not far-flung enough). Then they can bore you rigid with answers to questions you never even knew you wanted to ask. If you see what I mean.

Oops – your tiresome teacher's getting worryingly close. Don't panic! That's where this book is going to come in dead handy. Stick your nose in your copy and he won't even notice you're there. You hope. Besides, something even more exciting than you seems to have caught his attention. Oh no, he's talking to himself again…

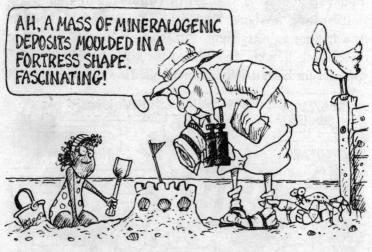

AH, A MASS OF MINERALOGENIC DEPOSITS MOULDED IN A FORTRESS SHAPE. FASCINATING!

Embarrassing, isn't it? But what on Earth is he mumbling on about? Have his brains turned to mush in the sun? Don't worry. Believe it or not, he's describing a SANDCASTLE! Yep, it really is as boringly normal as that. Luckily, not all Horrible Geography is as mind-bogglingly muddling as this. Actually, your tedious teacher is talking about cracking coasts – one of the most fascinating bits of geography ever.

And that's what this book is all about. From cavernous cliffs and sand-tastic sand dunes to whopping waves taller than your house, coasts and their freaky features crop up all over the world. In *Cracking Coasts*, you can…

• gawp at a coastline carved out by a giant

• dig for dazzling diamonds in the sand

• visit the hotel that fell off a cliff

• learn to talk like a cool surfer with Shelley, your coast guide.

Feel like finding out more? Why not leave your barmy teacher busy beach-combing and head into the next chapter? It's a cracking read. But here's a word of warning before you turn the page. The coast might look wonderfully warm and sunny – as if it wouldn't hurt even a teeny little fly. But don't be fooled by appearances. Even a lovely day by the seaside can suddenly turn nasty. Very nasty indeed…

SAILING TOO CLOSE TO THE WIND

20 July 1985, Florida, USA

It was just before 1 pm on a sunny, summer's afternoon. Anchored off the Florida coast, the crew of a small boat, called the *Dauntless*, watched anxiously as a diver's head bobbed up above the waves. They could hardly bear to watch. Could today finally be the day they'd been hoping for? Or would their dreams be dashed again? Every diver who'd searched the sea bed that day had returned to the boat empty-handed. So there was no reason to think things would be any different this time. Then the diver raised his mask…

"I've found it! I've found it!" he whooped. "The treasure! It's down there. And there's heaps of the stuff!"

The shell–shocked crew couldn't believe their ears. As they cheered and hugged one another, they hauled the delighted diver back on board. When he got his breath back, he described the amazing sight he'd seen.

"I was having a dig around in the sand," he gasped, "thinking I was getting nowhere. Then, all of a sudden, I felt something. It was solid and about the size of a shoe box, I guess. Anyway, I rummaged around a bit more and felt another, then another and another… When I scraped away the sand, it was a gold bar! There's a whole stack of them down there. And they must be worth a fortune."

11

And there was more… Down on the murky sea floor, the diver had discovered the worm-eaten wreck of a long-lost Spanish galleon, the *Atocha*, which had sunk off this treacherous coast centuries ago. But the glittering gold bars were only a paltry part of the ship's precious cargo. Before long, the astonished crew began hauling up an awesome collection of gold and silver coins, rings and chains, and priceless emeralds from the dark depths of the sea. Astonishingly, they'd uncovered the greatest sunken treasure trove ever.

For over 350 years, this tantalizing treasure had lain in the inky darkness, alongside the fish-picked bones of the sailors who'd drowned when the ship went down. But how on Earth had the treasure got there? How had such a great galleon ended up in its watery grave? Read on for the tragic true tale of the *Atocha*'s last voyage. Warning: if you get seasick just looking at a wave, you might want to skip the next bit. The water's about to get horribly choppy.

23 March 1622, Cadiz, Spain

Sails billowing in the breeze, the *Nuestra Senora de Atocha* ("Our Lord of Atocha") leaves Spain bound for the Caribbean. This magnificent galleon is one of a fleet of 28 treasure ships that make this voyage every year. On its outward journey across the Atlantic Ocean, the *Atocha* carries much-needed supplies of clothes, wine, tools and cooking equipment for the Spanish settlers in Central and South America. (Since the 1530s, Spain has claimed many of these lands for its own.) On its return, its hold will be filled with vast amounts of priceless gold, silver and gemstones from these far-off lands.

24 May 1622, Portobello, Panama

It's a risky journey at the best of times. So the ships don't leave until late spring when the worst of the winter storms are over and the sea is calm. Usually. At first, everything goes according to plan. After a smooth crossing, the fleet splits up to collect treasure from the different ports. The *Atocha* reaches Portobello in Panama. Trains of pack-horses are still trekking into the city, carrying treasure from Peru. Astonishingly, so much treasure pours into the port that it takes almost two months to record it and load the *Atocha*. Finally, on 22 July, the heavily laden *Atocha* is ready to sail for Havana in Cuba to join up with the rest of the fleet.

27 July–3 August 1622, Cartagena, Venezuela

On route to Havana, the *Atocha* makes an unexpected stop at Cartagena in Venezuela. There it picks up an extra cargo – thousands of exquisite emeralds bound for the coffers of the Spanish king. The delay could prove costly. When the *Atocha* finally sails for Cuba, it is already weeks behind schedule. And, alarmingly, the hazardous hurricane season is about to start.

22 August 1622, Havana, Cuba

Things go from bad to worse. Heavy seas and gale-force winds make sailing seriously risky. It takes the *Atocha* over two weeks to reach Havana, where it joins the other ships of the fleet. Between them, they carry a stash of treasure worth a staggering £300 million. Official records show that the *Atocha* alone carries a cargo of 150,000 gold and silver coins, over 1,000 gold and silver bars and tens of thousands of emeralds. Not to mention seriously valuable supplies of tobacco, rosewood, indigo (a kind of blue dye) and copper ingots. And with a number of wealthy Spanish nobles and merchants also on board, alongside the crew, the ship is dangerously overcrowded.

4 September 1622, still in Havana

Finally, on 4 September, the ill-fated fleet sets sail for Spain. The *Atocha* brings up the rear. It is heavily armed with 20 colossal cannons for fending off treasure-hungry pirate ships. But a far deadlier enemy lies in wait. It is now late in the hurricane season – far too late for ships to sail safely. Even the *Atocha*'s fearsome firepower will be no match for the violent storms that could soon be battering the ship. The fleet sets a course north towards Florida, USA. But even now the winds are picking up and they grow stronger and wilder throughout the night.

5 September 1622, Florida coast, USA

By daybreak, the seas are mountainous, whipped into gigantic waves by the howling wind. To the sailors' horror, the ships are heading straight into the path of a hurricane. Aboard the *Atocha*, the chief pilot lights a lantern as the sky grows as black as night and torrents of rain lash down. All day long, the ship takes an appalling pounding. The wind rips its sails to shreds and snap its masts as if they were matchsticks. As the ship tilts violently from side to side, frothing green water slops across its deck. Just before darkness, a veil of stinging sea-spray closes around the petrified passengers and crew. They watch in horror as the ship in front capsizes and sinks without trace.

That night, the wind shifts direction and the hurricane hurls the fleet further north towards the Florida coast ... and disaster. Here, the shoreline is fatally fringed with underwater reefs. If the ship hits these jagged chunks of coral, its fate will be sealed. For now, most of the terrified passengers and crew huddle below deck, praying for their lives. But nothing can save them. Slowly but surely, the *Atocha* is swept headlong to its doom.

6 September 1622, Florida coast, USA

Next day, a small ship is sent from the fleet to search for survivors. It's a thankless task. Of the *Atocha*'s 265 passengers and crew, 260 have drowned. Only five people – three crewmen and two slaves – are rescued alive, clinging to a mast for dear life. Here's how one of the shaken survivors might have reported his appalling ordeal:

Day was breaking and we could see the outline of the coast. The winds were terrible. They were driving us closer and closer to the shore... The captain ordered us to drop anchor to try to hold the ship off the reef. But we didn't stand a chance. Suddenly, a giant wave lifted the ship up, then smashed it down hard on the reef. The main mast snapped like a twig and the coral ripped great holes in the ship's side. Then water began pouring in and the ship started sinking. All around me, people were screaming and trying to keep their heads above the waves, but it was hopeless, hopeless. A few of us managed to cling to the stump of the mast. And then we waited to drown...

Treasure hunters

Immediately, salty old seadog, Gaspar de Vargas, was put in charge of searching for the *Atocha*'s lost treasure. He and his team of divers found the ship lying 18 metres down in the water. So far, so good. But exploring the wreck was a risky job. In the days before scuba-diving equipment was invented, the divers could only stay underwater for about five minutes at a time – as long as they could hold their breath. So they didn't have much time to spare. But when they reached the *Atocha*, they found the hatches into the cargo hold firmly locked. The only treasure they managed to rescue was two paltry cannons.

De Vargas headed back to Havana for more divers and tools. But when he returned to the wreck site, the *Atocha* was nowhere to be seen. The hurricane had stirred up the shifting sea bed and covered the ship with sand. Even so, de Vargas didn't give up. He set up camp on a nearby island and sent out boatload after boatload of divers to drag the sea bottom with hooks. Every time their hooks snagged on something, the divers plunged head first overboard.

But they always returned empty-handed and soon even gutsy de Vargas had to admit defeat and head back home to Spain.

As for the *Atocha*, despite many rumours, no one managed to track the ship down. Then, in the 1960s, intrepid American treasure hunter, Mel Fisher, took up the search once more. As a boy, young Mel had dreamed of treasure hunting and had even made his own diver's helmet so he could go exploring the murky lagoon by his home.

START PUMPING!

Later he went to work on his family's chicken farm until he earned enough money to open his own scuba-diving shop. And now his big chance had come. From an old Spanish document, he found a detailed description of where the *Atocha* had sunk, so he knew exactly where to look. He put together a team of expert divers and a boat called *Dauntless*. For years, the divers found nothing apart from a handful of coins. Often the weather was so appalling they had to call off the search. Then, in 1975, Fisher's son stumbled on the ship's nine cannons – the biggest clue so far. It felt like the *Atocha*'s treasure was tantalizingly close. And, on that sunny July day, Fisher and his long-suffering team made their stunning breakthrough. Back in his office, Fisher's radio crackled to life.

"WZG 9605. Unit 1, this is Unit 11," came the message from the *Dauntless*. "Put away the charts. We've got ourselves a treasure trove!"

Earth-shattering fact
Over the next few years, Fisher and his divers hauled up a hoard of treasure worth a staggering £350 million. Fortunately for Fisher, he had a boatload of high-tech gear to help him. The divers had sophisticated scuba gear (scuba is short for "self-contained underwater breathing apparatus"). So instead of having to hold their breath, they had portable air tanks strapped to their backs. Fisher also had sonar for sweeping the sea bed for clues. Sonar is a system that uses sound to detect objects underwater. Beeps of sounds bounce off the objects and send back echoes, which show up on an on-board screen. The plan was to use the sonar to detect the wreck, then to send the divers down. Trouble is, even sonar's not completely foolproof. It stumbled on a couple of bombs, hundreds of empty beer cans and even a clapped-out car before it finally tracked the Atocha *down.*

IS IT SPANISH?

Phew! That was a real roller-coaster of a ride. Bet you're glad to be safely back on dry land again. It's true, coasts can be horribly dangerous, but they're also fascinating places to be. So while you get your breath back, why not get to know more about cracking coasts? There are miles of coasts to choose from and they crop up all over the world. But what exactly are cracking coasts and how on Earth did they get there? Time to "coast" along in the next chapter and sea, sorry, see for yourself.

CROOKED COASTLINES

Forget boring geography books. Oh, you already have. The best way to find out about cracking coasts is to check one out for yourself. Go on, it won't bite. Some globe-trotting geographers think nothing of travelling halfway round the world to gawp at a really peachy beach. While you've only got to drag yourself out of your deck chair. Apart from tiresome teachers, what on Earth can you see? Miles and miles of sandy beach and white-tipped waves lapping on the shore? Or colossal caves and towering cliff-tops carved out of the rotten rock? One thing's for certain – there's much more to a coast than first meets the eye.

What on Earth are coasts?

Ask a horrible geographer to describe a coast and he'll probably start spouting some appalling gobbledygook like this:

Technically speaking, a coast's the space in which terrestrial environments influence marine environments and vice versa...

Bet you wish you'd never asked. But don't panic if it sounds like utter claptrap. What our long-winded friend really means to say is that a coast is a place where the land and sea meet. So why on Earth can't he simply say that? Yep, folks, coasts are places right on the edge.

Top ten crooked coasts

Look at any map of the world and you'll notice coasts snaking sneakily around islands and the edges of continents. Look closer and you'll quickly spot that there's not a single straight bit of coast to be seen. Yep, coasts are seriously crooked. In fact, there's about 440,000 kilometres of crooked coast on

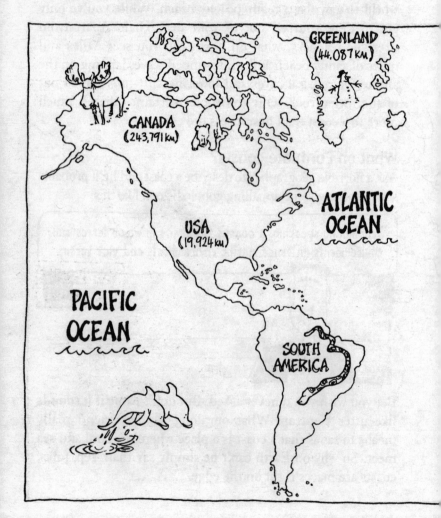

Earth. That's an awful lot of seashore. If you could straighten all the squiggles out, it would stretch a staggering 13 times around the equator (that's an imaginary line around the middle of the Earth). And guess what? It would take you a footsore 40 years to walk from one end to the other. On the other hand, you could stay at home and check out this map of the world's top ten longest coastlines instead.

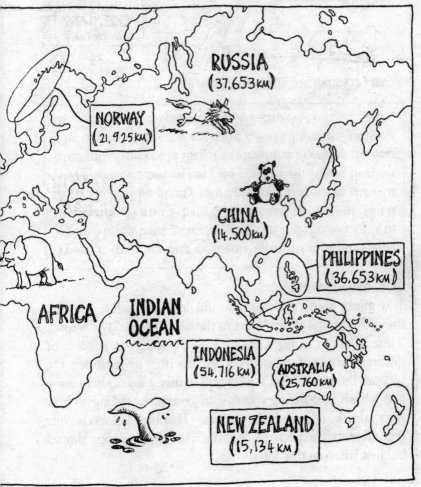

RUSSIA
(37,653 km)

NORWAY
(21,925 km)

CHINA
(14,500 km)

PHILIPPINES
(36,653 km)

AFRICA

INDIAN OCEAN

INDONESIA
(54,716 km)

AUSTRALIA
(25,760 km)

NEW ZEALAND
(15,134 km)

Teacher teaser

Is your teacher's coastal know-how all it's cracked up to be? Why not ask her this simple-sounding question.

PLEASE, MISS, WHERE DO PEOPLE IN MONGOLIA GO ON THEIR HOLIDAYS?

What on Earth are you talking about?

Answer: Your teacher probably hasn't the faintest clue where Mongolians go on holiday. But it definitely isn't to the seaside. With all that cracking coast to boast of, you'd think there'd be plenty to go around. But more than 40 land-locked countries have no coast at all. If you lived in Mongolia, you could forget a refreshing break by the sea. The closest coast's a staggering 2,400 kilometres away on the shores of the Yellow Sea in China.

Confusing coasts

You might think all coasts would look the same. I mean, they're all strips of land next to the sea. But you'd be wrong. Time to zoom in for a closer look. In fact, you get lots of different types of coasts. Ask any horrible geographer. On second thoughts, don't bother. Genius geographers have had a bash at splitting coasts into groups according to how they think coasts were made. Trouble is, even our argumentative experts can't agree what these groups should be. Just listen to this lot...

Coasts are either emergent or submergent. They always have been and they always will be.

Roughly translated, emergent coasts are created by the sea level falling or the land rising. The sea level fell during the last Ice Age, 18,000 years ago. So much water was locked up in glaciers and ice sheets that the sea was 100 metres lower ... uncovering loads of new coast. Other bits of coasts popped up when the ice sheets melted and the land underneath rose up. And it's the opposite for submergent coasts. They happen when the sea level rises or the land sinks. The sea level is rising because of global warming (check this out on page 120). And in places, the land is sinking because rivers aren't dumping enough sediment (that's rocks and soil) to build the land up. Got all that?

Stuff and nonsense. Coasts are either active or passive. What on Earth could be simpler than that?

Roughly translated, it's all down to plates. No, not the sort of plates you scoff your tea from. These pushy plates are gigantic pieces of the Earth's crust. Get this. The crust's the rocky surface of the Earth and the bit you play footie on. And it's cracked into seven monster (and lots of smaller) pieces called plates. But these crazy-paving plates don't just sit there, all nice and still. No way. They float about, ever so slowly, on the hot, gooey rock under the crust.

What's all this got to do with coasts? Well, an active coast crops up where the land and sea bed sit on different plates. These push and shove each other, setting off violent volcanoes and earthquakes. A passive coast is where the land and sea share the same plate. So things are nice and quiet. Normally.

What a load of twaddle. Coasts are high-energy or low-energy. Obviously.

Roughly translated, this depends on the size and strength of the waves breaking on a particular stretch of shoreline. For a high-energy coast, you need whopping waves crashing non stop against the shore. If your waves are just lapping gently, you'll end up with a low-energy kind of coast.

Cracking coast-to-coast guide

Heard enough? What's that? You weren't listening? Well, you can take your fingers out of your ears now. I SAID YOU CAN… All these tongue-twisting technical terms are fine if you're a brainy geography boffin, but you can forget all about them. The really interesting things about coasts are the bits you can actually see. Fancy a spot of sightseeing? Why not leave this lot squabbling and dip into the latest Horrible Geography: Coast-to-Coast Guide? It's full of *really* fascinating facts about coastal zones (that's coasts and the bits around them).

Name: MANGROVE SWAMPS

Location: Along tropical coasts

Coastal features:

• They're vast, squelchy swamps that form where tropical rivers flow into the sea. They only grow in warm places because mangrove plants can't stand the cold.

• They're named after mangrove trees. These brilliant bloomers are famous for having two kinds of roots. One sort grows in a tangle underwater and anchors the trees in the slimy mud. Otherwise, the tide would wash them away. The other sort poke out of the water and suck in air so the trees can breathe.

• Even though the mud's seriously salty and slippery, mangrove swamps are bursting with amazing wildlife. Fancy going on a swamp safari? Simply pick your swamp, hop in a boat and get paddling. Best not dangle your fingers in the water, though. However refreshing it feels. These steamy swamps are home to some horribly peckish crocodiles.

Mangrove swamps to check out: India/Bangladesh; Philippines; Thailand; South Pacific islands

Name: DELTAS
Location: Where some rivers flow into the sea
Coastal features:

• A delta's a muddlesome maze of streams and islands found at a river's mouth (that's the bit where the river flows into the sea). Here the river flows so slowly it can't lug its load of mud and sand along any more, so it dumps it. The tides wash some of the load out to sea, but the rest builds up new land, which the river has to branch out to flow round.

• Deltas got their name when an ancient Greek globe-trotter called Herodotus visited Egypt. He noticed the mouth of the River Nile was shaped like the Greek letter D, or Delta, which the ancient Greeks wrote like a triangle. Clever, eh?

• You also get pointy-shaped deltas and deltas shaped like a bent bow (officially, the Nile Delta is this shape). The Mississippi Delta in the USA is a bird's foot delta because it's got little branches sticking out like the toes on a bird's foot. Apparently.

Deltas to check out: Danube (Romania); Nile (Egypt); Mississippi (USA); Mekong (Vietnam)

Horrible Health Warning

Deltas are fantastic for farming because the soil's so fabulously fertile. So it's no wonder millions of people choose to live on deltas. Trouble is, the land's also fearfully flat and low-lying, so your fields could go under fast if the raging river floods.

YOU'RE LUCKY THE WATER ONLY CAME UP TO YOUR ANKLES!

I'M STANDING ON MY ROOF...

Take the gigantic Ganges-Brahmaputra delta in the Bay of Bengal. It covers an enormous 75,000 sq km. That's almost the same size as the whole of Austria. The delta is home to over 100 million people who rely on the land for farming. But it's a horribly risky place to live. In October 1988, the delta was hit by one of the fiercest floods in its history. This fatal flood drowned fields and crops, washed away buildings and left millions of people homeless.

Name: ESTUARIES

Location: Where some rivers flow into the sea

Coastal features:

• They're found at the mouths of rivers where salty seawater meets fresh river water and the tide mixes the two together. They're different from draining deltas because deltas aren't really ruffled by the tides. In case you were wondering.

• This mixing means that estuary water is oozing with goodness. So estuaries make brilliant nurseries for millions of baby fish and shellfish. In turn, these provide rich pickings for peckish birds and people.

• For centuries, seafaring humans have used estuaries as the perfect places to build harbours and ports. Some of the world's biggest cities have grown up around them. Take the Thames Estuary in England where the River Thames flows into the North Sea. Head upriver a bit and you'll end up in London.

Estuaries to check out: Thames Estuary (England); Chesapeake Bay (USA); Bay of Fundy (Canada)

Name: FJORDS (fee-ords)
Location: Along steep, mountainous coasts
Coastal features:

• A fjord's a long, jagged dent in the coastline. Fjords formed in steep-sided valleys gouged out by ancient glaciers. When the glistening glaciers melted, the fjords filled up with sea water.

• The longest fjord in the world is Scoresby Sund in Greenland. This groovy gash is a gobsmacking 350 km long.

• Fjords can be depressingly deep, plunging over 1,300 metres down. This makes it tricky for horrible geographers to get to the bottom of things. So scientists studying some icy Arctic fjords came up with a cunning plan. They fitted sensors to some whopping white whales and sent them in for a swim. Bet that made a whale of a splash. Signals from the sensors were picked up by satellites and sent to the scientists.

Fjords to check out: Sognefjord (Norway); Milford Sound (New Zealand); Seno Penguin (Chile)

Name: **CORAL REEFS**
Location: Along warm, tropical coasts
Coastal features:

• Incredibly, colossal coral reefs are built by puny polyps (tiny sea creatures related to jellyfish and sea anemones). Millions of them live together in groups. The polyps build hard, stony cases to stop their soft bodies getting squashed. When they die, layers of cases get left behind and make a reef.

• Coral reefs buzz with clownfish, butterfly fish, parrot fish, sea snakes, reef sharks, starfish, feather stars, giant clams, lionfish, sea slugs, octopuses... You get the picture.

• The Great Barrier Reef off north-east Australia is gigantic. It covers over 200,000 sq km and is over 2,000 km long. Coral grows ever-so slowly, at about the same rate as your fingernails. So to build a monster reef like this took about **18 MILLION** years.

Coral reefs to check out: Great Barrier Reef (Australia); Fijian Island (South Pacific Ocean); Red Sea (Indian Ocean)

Name: BARRIER ISLANDS
Location: Stretching along many coasts
Coastal features:

• These long, sandy islands run alongside a sixth of all the world's cracking coasts. They're separated from the mainland by lazily-lapping lagoons. The islands are constantly shifting as storms and waves reshape their shores.

• The islands can be hundreds of kilometres long but only tens of metres wide. But in places, the sand piles up into high-rise heaps up to 100 metres tall.

• Horrible geographers aren't sure how barrier islands began. Some think they were once large sandbars out at sea that the waves wafted towards the shore. Others reckon they're the remains of old beaches that drowned when the ice melted at the end of the last Ice Age.

Barrier islands to check out: Cape Hatteras (North Carolina USA); Galveston Island (USA); Friesian Islands (Netherlands, Germany); Abidjan (Ivory Coast)

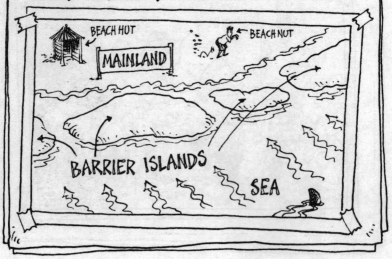

Baffling bays

You'll be pleased to know that not all crooked coasts will give you goose-pimples. Though sneak a peek at any map of the world and you're sure to spot plenty of freaky coastal features with strange-sounding names. Take baffling bays*, for starters. Some bays are named after ghastly geographical features or the peculiar plants and animals that live there. Or the long-suffering sailors who first sailed into them. So do any of these bays really live up their baffling names? Try this quirky quiz to find out the story behind some of them.

*By the way, a bay's an enormous dent in the coastline that the sea has filled in. But don't get your bays mixed up with your gulfs and coves. A gulf's bigger than a bay and it's got more land around it. A cove's like a mini bay. Bet that's as clear as mud.

Are the following true or false?

1 Baffin Bay is named after ace explorer William Baffin.
TRUE/FALSE?

2 Shark Bay got its name because it's shark-shaped.
TRUE/FALSE?

3 Repulse Bay got its name because it's so repulsive.
TRUE/FALSE?

4 Chesapeake Bay means "Great Shellfish Bay".
TRUE/FALSE?

5 Botany Bay is named after its lovely, green bloomers.
TRUE/FALSE?

SHE MEANS PLANTS!

OOOPS!

Answers:
1 TRUE. Bracing Baffin Bay lies between the icy Arctic and North Atlantic Oceans. For most of the year, ships can't sail across it because it's infested with hazardous icebergs. It's named after ace British explorer William

Baffin (1584–1622). Well, William Bay didn't have quite the same ring. Baffled Baffin stumbled on the bay by accident in 1616, while he was searching for a new trade route across the frozen far north to the east.

2 FALSE. It's not a bad guess, but the true answer is that Shark Bay in Australia got its snappy name because it's, er, chock-full of sharks. But that's not all this beautiful bay's famous for. It's also home to thousands of dugongs (a dugong's a large, lumpy sea mammal, sometimes called a sea cow) and dolphins, not to mention over 300 kinds of fish (apart from sharks). Not to mention sensational Shell Beach, which is made up of billions of minuscule sea shells.

3 FALSE. Repulsive means horrible. But in fact, Repulse Bay in Hong Kong is quite the opposite of that. It's so stunningly scenic, that it has become one of the most expensive places on Earth to live. If you fancy a high-rise home in this neck of the woods, you'd better start saving up. Renting a posh apartment overlooking the bay will set you back a whopping £650,000 a month! So how on Earth did the bay get its off-putting name? A story goes that it dates back to the 19th century when navy ships repulsed, or drove off, pirates attacking the bay. And the name stuck.

NO MORE REPULSIVE JOKES THEN

WHAT?

4 TRUE. In the local Indian language, the word Chesapeake means "great shellfish" and the bay's famous for its clams, oysters and blue crabs. Bucketloads of these tasty shellfish are caught in the bay every year. Today, overfishing and pollution have cut down the numbers of shellfish being caught. But in the past, people could pop out and scoop them up in frying pans!

ARGH! THE GREAT FRYING PAN OF DOOM!

5 TRUE. But not the sort of bloomers your dear old granny pegs out on her washing line! This bay is in Australia and it's named after its amazing plants. (Botany means the study of plants.) The first Europeans to visit the bay were trail-blazing British explorer James Cook and his crew in 1770. We don't know if Cook had green fingers. But handily, he'd got top botanist, Joseph Banks (1743–1820) on board. And Banks was potty about plants. When he wasn't being seasick, he spent hours leafing through botany books. And he collected so many samples of plants that he needed four servants to help him sort them all out. (Luckily, Banks was filthy rich so he'd brought along some of his servants from home.)

Here's what Banks's botanical notebook might have looked like...

MY NOTEBOOK (April 1770)
By Joseph Banks

Day 1

A piece of luck! We've found a beautiful bay to anchor in, and – get this – every hill for miles around seems to be jam-packed with plants and trees. I'm sooo excited (when I'm not feeling horribly seasick). I can't wait to go ashore. I've been cooped up in my cabin for weeks. As soon as the boat's ready, I'm off. I don't care what old Cook says. Plants, here I come... I hope I find something really earth-shattering. This trip's costing me a fortune.

PS We've called the bay Stingray Bay because of all the stingrays we've seen. By the way, stingrays are seriously scrummy. We had stingray steak for tea today and tomorrow it's stingray soup for lunch. Yummy.

Stingray or lunch!

Days 2-7

What a week! Every day, Daniel (my trusty assistant) and I have been ashore and had a good look round. I was right. There are plants EVERYWHERE! We've collected so many, we're running out of room for them on the ship. Trouble is, most of the plants are already wilting and there's no way they'll last until we get home. Before they rot, I've got the ship's artist working day and night sketching as many as he can. (Until he gets round to them, we've wrapped them in damp cloths to keep them fresh.) Unfortunately, he's only got time to draw them in black and white so he'll have to colour them in later on.

Pressed flower

Squashed bug!

breakfast!

Anyway, the brilliant news is that we keep accidentally discovering brand-new kinds of plants. In fact, the plants round here are so peculiar, they've never been seen by Europeans before. I can't wait to tell the folks back home. They'll go green with envy! He! He!

PS We've decided to name the bay Botany Bay instead because of all the plants we've found. And a bit of the bay's now called "Cape Banks" after, well, me!

Day 8
Oh well, all good things must come to an end. It's a bloomin' lovely spot and I could have stayed here for weeks. But the Captain's keen to set sail. Still, I've got plenty of colouring in to keep me busy. If only I didn't feel so, er, hang on, I'll be back in a tick...

Back home, plant-mad Banks was treated like a superstar and showered with titles and honours. His colossal plant collection became the talk of the botanical world and he was made boss of Britain's Kew Gardens. He even had several of the plants he'd found named after him. Unfortunately, all this fame and fortune went straight to Banks's head. He became so horribly vain and boastful that fed-up Captain Cook refused to take him on his next voyage.

So you've got to know your cracking coast and that's all very well, you might say. Coasts may be lovely to look at but aren't they dull as ditchwater? After all, what on Earth does a coast actually do, except lounge around lazily by the sea? Well, you couldn't be more wrong. Just like you in a ghastly geography lesson, coasts simply can't stay still. Just when you thought you'd got coasts cracked, they go and change dramatically. Read on if you don't believe me.

SHIFTING SHORES

Like your beach-combing geography teacher, coasts are seriously shifty. How come? Well, they're constantly changing shape. Look carefully at your cracking coast. What can you see? You'll notice the coast never looks exactly the same on two days running. Some of these changes happen overnight. I mean, one day the shore might be seaweed-free … the next, the sea's covered it in slimy stuff. Other changes take much longer. It takes years and years for the sea to carve out a cliff-side cave. So what on Earth is going on? Let's start with some breaking news about wild waves…

What on Earth are waves?

1 Waves are gigantic ripples of water that the wind whips up as it blows across the sea. And they make the going horribly choppy. But waves only ruffle the surface of the sea. Deep down you won't feel a thing. So if you're planning a boat trip in stormy weather, try hitching a lift in a submarine instead. Otherwise you might be in for a sickeningly bumpy ride.

SUB-BOARDING!

The shell-shocked crew of the USS *Ramapo* learned about bumpy rides the hard way. In 1933, their ship was rocked by a whopping wave 34 metres tall (that's about five times as high as your house). The size of a wave depends on the wild wind. The stronger the wind and the longer it blows, the bigger the waves will be. It must have been a particularly stormy day.

Earth-shattering fact
At least the rocking Ramapo *wasn't sailing across Lituya Bay in Alaska on 9 July 1958, so it missed the lethal landslide set off by a colossal earthquake. The landslide hurled millions of tonnes of rock into the sea, creating a monster wave which washed over 500 METRES up the opposite cliff. Then the whopping wave sped down the bay, picked up a bunch of fishing boats and washed them out to sea. (OK, so strictly speaking it wasn't a wave because it wasn't caused by the wind – but talk about making a splash!)*

WAVE! WAVE!

WHO TO?

3 Ever wondered how waves are measured? Well, here's your chance to find out. Grab yourself a (waterproof) tape measure and get ready to take the plunge. Better still, send your teacher, then you won't have to get soaking wet. She'll need to measure the distance between the trough (that's the lowest bit of the wave) and the crest (that's the highest bit) to tot up the woeful wave's height.

YOU CAN WAVE GOODBYE TO NO HOMEWORK!

4 The way waves eventually crash on to the shore is called "breaking". Yep, the wobbly waves reach breaking point. (Bet your teacher knows that feeling. If she ever dries out.) What happens is this:

a) Out at sea, the waves are small and low.

b) As they near the shore, the water gets shallower...

46

c) ...and the waves start to slow down*.

d) The waves bunch up and get taller...

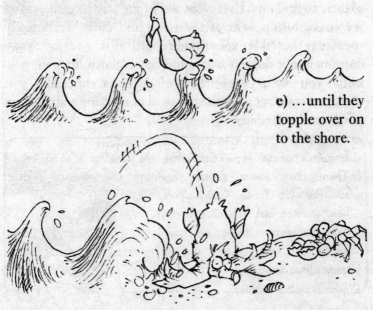

e) ...until they topple over on to the shore.

*The waves slow down because of friction. That's a force which tries to stop one thing (the waves) moving past another thing (the sea bed). Horrible geographers call this "feeling the bottom". Try telling that to your teacher.

5 The waves you see breaking on the coast may have travelled thousands of kilometres to get there. But that's not the end of their soggy story. Every day, walloping waves crash against the coast, eating away at the rocks and cliffs. Technically speaking, horrible geographers call this wearing away erosion, and it doesn't half grind coasts down. I mean, how would you like having bucketloads of water chucked at you all day, every day? And all this erosion's having a shattering effect on the seashore.

Erosion's worse in winter when the weather's stormier. Then the waves smash against the shore with ENORMOUS force. Geographers have worked out it's like having 50 elephants sitting on your knee. Well, they didn't put it quite like that.

Erosion – the shattering story

Waves may look woefully wet but don't be fooled by appearances. They're horribly powerful. So powerful that they can eat away at chunks of solid rock and completely change the face of the coast. But it's not just the watery bits of waves that do the damage. Waves lug along loads of sand and pebbles that give them their cutting edge. So how do the waves wear the crumbling coast down? Time to call in the experts…

SMASH, CRASH & BATTER LTD
DEMOLITION EXPERTS
FOR HIRE

Tired of gawping at the same old coastline? Fed up with cliffs blocking your sea view? Fancy giving your clapped-out coast a makeover?

Why not call in our crack squad of demolition experts? They'll soon knock your coast into a brand-new shape for you. What's more, we offer a year-round service with 24-hour call-out.

Choose from our cutting-edge range of services:

• **OPTION 1:** We'll hurl bucketloads of waves against your cliffs so the water traps tiny pockets of air inside cracks in the rocks. Eventually, the trapped air will put the rotten rocks under so much pressure, they'll start to fall apart at the seams. We experts call this hydraulic (high-draw-lick) erosion, and it's our most popular option by miles.

• **OPTION 2**: Choose this option and we'll make sure the waves pick up tonnes of sand, rock and boulders. Next time they hit the coast, they'll work like a gigantic sheet of sandpaper and scrape your coast into shape. This is called abrasion in the trade. It's brilliant for attacking cliff bottoms, leaving the cliffs dangerously top-heavy.

• **OPTION 3**: We'll take rocks and boulders that have already broken off your cliffs and chuck them into the sea. Then the waves can get to work grinding them up into teenier and teenier pieces. Technically speaking, this erosion option's called attrition and it's a cracking way of getting the job done.

• **OPTION 4**: And finally, this option will see us spraying your coast with sea water so the acid in it attacks the rocks and they dissolve. What could be simpler than that? We experts call this corrosion. By the way, we'd recommend using slightly warm seawater so we might have to wait for a sunny day. Warm water works faster than cold.

SPECIAL OFFER:

You can mix and match as many of our options as you like – at no extra cost. Actually, you may as well. They'll happen naturally at the same time anyway.

OPTIONAL EXTRAS:

As a fabulous finishing touch, why not try adding a handful of crabs or starfish? These cracking creatures dig their burrows in the rocks, leaving a pretty, honeycombed pattern behind. Please ask our experts if you're interested.

What one satisfied customer said:
"I went for the hydraulic option and it worked swimmingly. My coast used to be bland and boring but now it's collapsing around my ears."

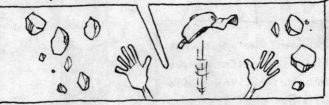

SMALL PRINT:

Cracking results are guaranteed, but don't blame us if it takes some time. The freaky features you're about to check out don't happen overnight. They take hundreds or even thousands of years. It depends on what kind of rock your cliff's made from.

Cracking coastal features

So now you know how earth-shattering erosion works, but what shape do you want your shoreline to be? To find out about some of the freaky features you'll find along the coast, why not join Shelley for a bracing cliff-top walk?

Hi, folks, Shelley here, welcoming you on my cracking coastal walk. Hope you've got your cameras handy. You're in for some breathtaking views. But before we get going, there's something you should know. Please stick closely to the path, won't you? This walk's a real cliffhanger and I don't want anyone falling off the edge. OK, is everyone ready for a high-rise stroll?

Headland: See that high bit of rock sticking out into the sea? With cliffs on either side? It's called a headland and it happens when the waves eat away at soft rock, leaving hard rock behind. Yes, you can look down now.

Cliff: Like headlands, high-rise cliffs are carved into shape by the waves. These cliffs might seem horribly high to you but they're actually quite paltry. To check out the world's highest sea cliffs, you'd need to head south to Hawaii. It's a whole kilometre from the cliff top to the sea below. What's that, you're feeling dizzy?

HEADLAND

CLIFF

SEA CAVES

Sea cave: If you look down, you'll see a couple of caves. That's right, lad, over there. They form when the waves wear away at cracks in the headland, carving them into gaping holes. If anyone fancies a closer look, there's a boat trip leaving later.

Arch: If you get two caves on either side of a headland, the sea sometimes punches a hole in between. Anyone know what the freaky feature that's left is called? No? Oh dear, never mind – the answer's an arch.

STACK
(Well, soon will be)

ARCH

STUMP

Sea stack: You might want to move to your left, miss. Watch out, miss, that's your right. If the arch you're standing on collapses, you'll be left stranded out at sea on top of a large pillar of rock called a stack. Stacks make perfect perches for sea birds, but you wouldn't want to be scared of heights. Two tourists in Australia had the shock of their lives when the arch they were standing on collapsed suddenly. Luckily, a passing helicopter picked them up. It's OK, this arch's rock solid. I think.

Stump: Over years and years, the waves pound against the rocks at the bottom of the stack until the cracking stack slumps into the sea. All that's left is the stack's rocky stump. But even stumps have their uses. If you're stumped for somewhere to locate your lighthouse, a stump's the perfect place to pick.

Blowhole: If waves smash through the roof of a sea cave, the water spurts up through a blowhole. Yes, lad, like the one on top of a whale's head. Sort of. Oh dear, you'd better have a sit-down. That must have given you quite a shock.

BLOWHOLE

Collapsing cliffs

As you've seen, in some places erosion's having a crushing effect on the coast. So if you're planning a seaside break, pick your seaside carefully. Picture the scene. You've just arrived at your cliff-top hotel at the start of your summer holiday. You've unpacked your bucket and spade and you're about to head off for the beach. Suddenly, your hotel starts lurching alarmingly. Next thing you know, your hotel is hurtling down the crumbling cliff. Sounds too crackpot to be true? Well, that's exactly what happened to some horrified holiday-makers in 1993. Here's how the *Daily Globe* might have reported this earth-moving event.

SCARBOROUGH ENGLAND

Gobsmacked guests at the Holbeck Hall Hotel are still reeling from the shock of seeing their hotel slump into the sea. The town's top hotel, the Holbeck Hall, had perched daintily on the cliff top for over 100 years. People have been flocking to it for years for its breathtaking views across the bay. Today, the hotel lies in tatters, sprawled halfway down the cliff.

The cracks began to show a week ago. First, the hotel's rose garden crashed over the edge of the cliff and thousands of tonnes of rock and soil slipped into the sea. Then the conservatory started tilting precariously and cracks opened up in the car park. Soon, the hotel itself was teetering on the edge of the crumbling cliff.

The hotel's 80 guests and staff were ordered to leave for their own safety and the police were busy keeping curious onlookers at bay. Astonishingly, no one was injured but one guest gave our reporter this dramatic eyewitness account:

"I was just looking out of the window," he told us, "when I noticed the lawn was moving right in front of the hotel. Then I found my door jammed shut and cracks started running down my bedroom walls. It's a holiday I'll never forget. When I asked for a room with a sea view, I never dreamt it would be this close."

Experts are now trying to get to the bottom of what caused the hotel's dramatic collapse. It's thought that a combination of factors was to blame. The cliffs around the town have been cracking up for hundreds of years, eaten away by the stormy winter seas. And it's left the cliffs deeply unstable. On top of this, we've had months of heavy rain. This is thought to have set off the alarming landslide that sent the hotel slithering into the bay. And it was all downhill from then on.

Half of the collapsing hotel is still hovering dangerously on the edge of the cliff. Experts reckon it will only be a matter of days before it finally goes over the top. More likely, it will have to be demolished before that happens. Meanwhile, visitors have been pouring into the town to witness the hotel's last stand. Most were sad to see the hotel go.

"I've got a lot to thank that hotel for," one local shopkeeper told us. "Me 'Disaster Strikes' T-shirts have been selling like hot cakes all week."

Building beaches

With all those waves chomping away at the cracking coast, it's a wonder there's any coast left at all. But it's not all bad news. Waves aren't just wearing the coast down. In some places, they're actually building balmy beaches up. Yep, waves are master builders. If you thought beaches were simply for sunbathing, you might be in for a surprise. Here's a step-by-step guide to building a beach, and it's packed with gritty beach facts...

Get someone to think of a beach and they'll most likely describe miles and miles of golden sand. Which is lovely for lounging about on. But beaches aren't always like that. In fact, only about a quarter of beaches are sandy. The rest are covered in piles of pebbles, or even in slices of ice. Not quite so suitable for sunbathing.

Six shore-fire steps to building a sandy beach

1 *Pick a suitable spot*. It's best to steer clear of places where the wind's blowing a gale. That's because you need the waves to lap quite gently. Otherwise they'll wash away more beach-building material than they'll wash ashore. A sheltered bay is ideal.

2 *Let the waves get to work*. You want the waves to dump their loads of rocks and stones on to the shore. (Geographers call this deposition.) But where does all this beach-building stuff come from? The answer is most of it's washed into the sea by rivers or chipped off the cliffs by waves.

3 *Now smother the beach with sand*. Over millions of years, the waves smash rocks and stones to smithereens. Any minuscule fragments between 0.2 and 2 millimetres wide are called sand grains. But don't bother trying to count them. There are billions and billions on a beach. Sand isn't always sandy coloured. It depends what kind of rock it's made from. If the sand's greeny-grey or black, it's made from volcanic rock. So mind you don't toast your toes. If it's pretty pinkish-white, it isn't made from crunched-up rock at all. It's made from countless crushed seashells and chunks of coral.

Earth-shattering fact
You're strolling along the beach, whistling happily. Suddenly ... the sand joins in! Nope, you're not hearing things. The sand's started whistling! But you'll have to listen carefully. It's a horribly soft, squeaky sound. So what on Earth is going on? Geographers reckon the whistling starts when very fine grains of sand rub together, especially when the weather's dry. And guess who sets the sand off? You do, when you stomp along the beach.

4 *Shuffle the sand about a bit*. Beaches don't just lie there whistling. Now that would get boring. On some beaches, the sand's constantly being shuffled along the coast by what geographers call longshore drift. What happens is this. The waves break on the beach at an angle. Then they wash straight back into the sea again, shifting the sand along the shore in a pattern of gigantic zig-zags. Wakey, wakey. You'd drifted off. Here's a handy diagram to set you straight about longshore drift.

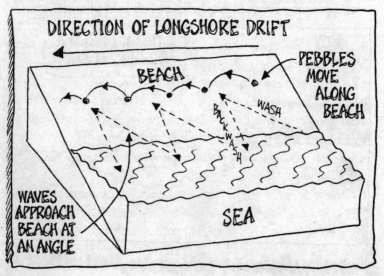

DIRECTION OF LONGSHORE DRIFT

BEACH

PEBBLES MOVE ALONG BEACH

WASH

BACKWASH

WAVES APPROACH BEACH AT AN ANGLE

SEA

5 *Knock your beach into shape*. So your sand's slowly drifting along, when the coastline suddenly goes and changes direction. If the sand carries on drifting, you might end up with a sticky-out bit of beach called a spit. You'll be able to spot your spit easily. Look out for the hook on the end (that's where the wind's blown the sand right around the bend). Sometimes a spit grows right across a bay, linking two headlands. Then it's called a bar. Or a spit joins an island to the mainland. Then it's called a tombolo. ("Tombolo" comes from a Latin word which means pile. So you see, even the ancient Romans must have had holidays by the beach.)

6 *Add a few sand dunes*. They're rippling piles of sand blown into shape by the wind. Here's what happens:

a) The wind blows the sand along the beach.

b) If it meets an obstacle like a clump of seaweed or driftwood, the wind slows down and drops its sandy load.

c) Then the sand settles and starts to pile up.

d) Soon, plants take root in the dune and stop the sand blowing away.

By the way, you might not want to hang around to watch. For starters, some sand dunes are enormous, growing over 30 metres high. And some are ancient. The dead old dunes along the Skeleton Coast are reckoned to have been growing for at least 130 million years.

The tide is turning

While you're waiting for your dune to start sprouting, mind you don't get swept out to sea by the tides. Apart from waves, tides are particularly powerful in shaping the seashore. I mean, one minute you've got loads of beach to lounge about on. The next, most of the bloomin' beach is smothered by sea. Want to know more about turning tides but in too much of a twist to ask? Don't worry. Here's Shelley back from her coast-to-coast walk to explain the ins and outs.

Q: Tides, eh? They sound seriously wet?

A: It depends. Tides are the way the sea rises and floods on to the shore. (The posh word for this is rising.) Then it flows out again. (The posh word for this is ebbing.) It's high tide when the water's in and low tide when it's out. But if you stand high enough up on the beach, you might avoid a soaking.

Q: Er, right. So how often do tides happen, then?

A: It varies. But in most places, they happen twice a day. Every day.

Q: Mmm, I see. But what actually makes the tide turn?

A: Hmm, that's a tricky question. Tides are mainly caused by the moon's gravity (that's a force that pulls things together. It's the Earth's gravity that keeps your feet on the ground). It pulls the oceans closest to the moon into a massive watery bulge. Are you with me so far?

Q: Er, sort of. Is that all?

A: Nope. This bulge needs balancing out. Luckily, the Earth is spinning on its axis (that's an imaginary line running down its middle). As it spins, it pulls the oceans on the other side into another monster bulge.

Q: Blimey. Is there anything else to blame?

A: Well, the sun sometimes gets in on the action. Twice a month, the sun and moon pull in a straight line. Then you get very high high tides and very low low tides. (Confusingly, they're called spring tides.) And twice a month, the sun and moon pull at right angles. Then you get high low tides and low high tides. (They're known as neap tides.) You see?

SPRING TIDE

NEAP TIDE

Q: Where do the highest tides happen?

A: In the Bay of Fundy, Canada. The difference between high tide and low tide is a massive 17 metres. They're the highest tides on Earth. But you can forget all about gravity. Legend says they're caused by a whopping whale splashing about in the water. But head for the sunny Mediterranean and you'll hardly notice the tides turning at all because the sea's so small and almost surrounded by land. Any more questions?

Q: You know loads about tides, miss. Are you a tidal bore?

A: Er, nope. A tidal bore's a monster wave that rushes up a river from the sea, washed in on the incoming tide. In some places, fishermen hitch lifts on bores to get them from A to B. Bet they don't think that's boring.

One thing's for certain. Never mind if it's waves or tidal bores, all this to-ing and fro-ing can be horribly unsettling. Especially if you happen to be a small sea creature that's set up home on the shifting shore. For these hardy seashore settlers, it really is make or break time…

CRACKING COASTAL WILDLIFE

You might think that living by the sea would be a doddle. Like going on a very long holiday. I mean, just think of all those lazy seaside strolls, listening to the soothing lapping of the waves. Bliss. But enjoy it while you can. Things can quickly turn nasty. Very nasty indeed. Whopping waves, turning tides and shifting sands make cracking coasts perilous places to live. Imagine you're a coastal creature searching for somewhere to call home, sweet home. Here are just some of the risks you'd run:

• Being soaked to the skin when the tide comes in

• Being left high and dry when the tide goes out

• Being swept out to sea by the waves and tides

Seashore survival

As well as this there's the tricky business of finding enough food to eat, oxygen to breathe and a safe place to shelter. (Come to think of it, you need all these things too.) You might think you've got it tough when your mum nags you to tidy your bedroom again. But that's nothing compared to living on the edge. There the going's seriously tough and cracking coastal creatures have to be hardy to survive. Oddly, despite the roller-coaster conditions, hundreds of hardy animals wouldn't live anywhere else. So how on Earth do they do it without being waterlogged or washed away? What's that? You haven't got the soggiest, sorry, foggiest? Don't worry. Shelley's favourite cousin, Sandy C. Shore has spent years studying seashore life. She's put together this cracking seashore survival handbook and it's packed with sneaky survival tips.

By the way, some of these tips are so top-secret that even your clever-clogs teacher won't have heard of them. So don't go telling everyone. After all, for the creatures in question, these helpful hints may be a matter of life or death. And you never know who's listening.

Seashore Survival Handbook (TOP secret) by Sandy C. Shore

Scampering mudskippers

Mudskippers are odd-looking fish that hang out in mangrove swamps. But get this. When the tide goes out, they skip across the mud using their tails like springs. It's true. Talk about fish out of water. And there's more. Normally, fish breathe oxygen  dissolved in the water through slitty gills in the sides of their heads. Not your sneaky mudskipper. This feisty fish can also breathe through its damp, fishy skin. So even when the tide's out, it gets enough oxygen. A really neat trick if you can pull it off. By the way, a mudskipper can turn its big, bulging eyes to look in any direction in case there's a tasty snack of flies about. Imagine how useful that would be, having eyes in the back of your head.

Sandy's survival rating: *****A survival superstar.

Burrowing lugworms

Lugworms don't just lounge about lazily as the tide goes out. Oh no. These cunning creatures dig burrows in the soggy sand to stop their soft bodies drying out. A simple but brilliant survival strategy. A lugworm's burrow is U-shaped. The worm stuffs sand into one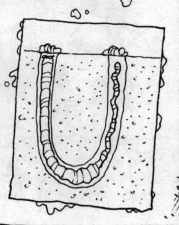

end then sucks water in through the sand. The sand works like a sieve and filters tiny specks of food from the water for the worm to scoff. Now that's what I call a gutsy character. You might not want a lugworm round for lunch, though. Its table manners are terrible. Every hour or so, it squeezes any left-over sand out of its body and pushes it to the surface. So, the curly squiggles of sand you see on the beach are actually, yep, you've guessed it … piles of lugworm poo!

*Sandy's survival rating: **** Dead clever but disgusting.*

Ingenious iguanas

This sea-loving lizard's a real tough cookie. For a start, it lives on the windswept shores of the wild Galapagos Islands in the Pacific Ocean. Most of the time it hangs out on land. But if it's feeling peckish, it braves the pounding waves and chilly water to munch seaweed growing on the slippery rocks. Luckily for the plucky lizard, it's got special claws for clinging on. So it can stuff its face with seaweed without getting swept off its feet. And it's a brilliant swimmer, using its long, flat tail like a paddle. Trouble is, this watery lifestyle has one really deadly drawback. Hanging out on the rocks makes this lunch-eating lizard a tasty snack for passing sharks.

*Sandy's survival rating: *** A brave but risky strategy.*

House-hunting hermit crab

Most crabs have shells to protect their soft, squishy bodies and to call home, sweet home. Except for the homeless hermit crab. Is it bothered? Is it, heck! The crab simply grabs an empty shell and sets up home in it. Whelk or periwinkle shells suit it best. And when the crab grows too big for its shell, it simply goes house-hunting again. But the crab doesn't live alone. Sea anemones sometimes hitch lifts on its shell. So what's in it for them? Well, the

sneaky anemones get to nibble on the crab's leftover food, and the crab gets extra protection from the anemone's stinging tentacles. And guess what? When the cunning crab moves shell, the anemone moves in with it.

Sandy's survival rating: ****A cracking case of teamwork.

Gripping goose barnacles

When it comes to getting a grip, you can't beat a goose barnacle. These crunchy crustaceans are masters at clinging on for dear life. What's more, they're not fussy. They'll cling on to

anything – rocks, glass bottles, ships' bottoms, and even wandering whales. How's that for a horribly handy way of getting about? How do the bean-sized barnacles stick at it? Simple, really. They squeeze out gooey globules of glue from their bodies. By the way, these clinging creatures got their name because their long stalks looked a bit like geese necks. OK, so you'll have to use your imagination for this bit. Some potty people even thought barnacles grew up and turned into geese!

Sandy's survival rating: ***** Goose barnacles really stick out.

Five freaky shellfish facts

Ask someone to describe a seashell and they'll probably go on and on about the pretty little shells you pick up on a seashore stroll. But don't be fooled. The shellfish that live inside these shiny shells have some truly horrible habits. For a start, they're not really fish. Strictly speaking, creatures like cockles, clams, limpets and sea snails are known as molluscs. And their shells aren't simply for show. They're for protecting the molluscs' soft, squishy bodies from peckish crabs and birds. Could you be a cracking conchologist*? Try this quick shellfish quiz to find out.

A conchologist is a scientist who studies seashells. "Conch" comes from an Ancient Greek word for shellfish. It's also the natty name of a sea snail with a spiral-shaped shell.

73

1 Limpets cling on to rocks by their fingertips. TRUE/FALSE

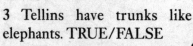

2 Mussels have hairy beards. TRUE/FALSE

3 Tellins have trunks like elephants. TRUE/FALSE

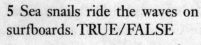

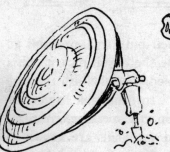

4 Piddocks can drill through solid rock. TRUE/FALSE

5 Sea snails ride the waves on surfboards. TRUE/FALSE

Answers:
1 FALSE. Limpets don't have fingers, silly. They cling on to rocks with their big ... feet! This way these sure-footed molluscs can get such a tight grip that even the wildest waves can't wash them off. That leaves the locked-on limpet

to graze happily on tiny plants called algae growing on the rocks. The only time an unlucky limpet comes unstuck is when a sneaky starfish slides it off sideways for supper.

2 TRUE. Mussels spend most of their lives clinging to rocks … by their beards. Yep, it's true! But bristling mussel beards aren't made from anything as boring as hair. They're actually made from clumps of soft, sticky threads. Stranger still, these threads don't sprout from a mussel's chin, like an ordinary beard. They're squeezed out of its fleshy foot and go hard when they hit the sea water. Weird or what?

3 TRUE. Tellins live on shifty sandy shores where there's nothing solid to hang on to. So these molluscs like to hide away in beach-front burrows. When it's feeling peckish, the tellin sticks its trunk-like tube out of its burrow like a mini vacuum cleaner, and sucks up minuscule scraps of food. Fish sometimes nibble the tip of the tellin's tube but it soon grows back again. Has the tellin got any other tricks up its shell? That would be tellin'.

4 TRUE. Piddocks are probably the most boring molluscs of all, but not because they're deadly dull. Using its shell like a drill bit, a piddock bores holes in solid rock. How on Earth does it do that? The answer is each half of its shell is fringed with rows of sharp teeth, which the pulverizing piddock uses to grind out a tunnel. Some piddock burrows can be 1 metre long. Not bad going for a mollusc that's only around twice as long as your little finger.

5 TRUE. Normally a sea snail lies buried in the sand. But when the tide comes in, it sucks water into its foot and uses it like a surfboard to ride the waves up the beach. As soon as the snail sniffs out a snack (stranded jellyfish are its favourite), it pulls in its surfboard and tucks straight in. Afterwards, it hitches a lift back to its burrow on the out-going waves.

Earth-shattering fact
Horseshoe crabs haven't anything to do with crunchy crabs and they're not really horseshoe-shaped either. In fact, these confusing creatures are related to spiders and scorpions – and they look like giant frying pans. The crabs spend most of the year out at sea looking for food.
But every spring, hundreds of thousands of them clamber on to the beach and lay their eggs in holes in the sand. When the baby crabs hatch out, they have to dash back to the sea before seagulls gobble them up.

Sensational seashore bloomers

For seashore plants, life's no picnic either. It's tough to take root in the shifting sands and they're constantly being battered by the wind and waves. So it's amazing that plenty of plucky plants still sprout along the cracking coast. Planning to plant up your own stretch of coastline but confused about which plants to choose? Don't worry, help is at hand. Here's our cracking coasts gardening guide for you to leaf through. We've picked a blooming lovely selection of plants that are pretty *and* practical. And we've thrown in some top planting tips, too.

Name: GIANT KELP

Description: A gigantic type of seaweed with long, leathery fronds. Grows up to 100 metres long.

Ideal position: Offshore, along rocky coasts

Planting tips: You'll need some sizeable sea-bed rocks for your kelp to cling on to. But then you can leave it alone to bloom. It's one of the fastest-growing plants on the planet and can grow over a metre IN A SINGLE DAY. So you'll need to give it plenty of room. Plant it up in clumps and you'll soon have a fabulous underwater forest. You'll find that the fronds grow up to the sunny sea surface (plants use sunlight to make their food). But don't bother tying them to sticks. They're covered in little air-filled bubbles so they'll keep bobbing upright in the water anyway.

Apart from being brilliant bloomers, giant kelp fronds are horribly useful. Especially if you're a sleepy sea otter. Before they nod off, sea otters in California, USA, wrap streaming strands of kelp around their bodies to stop them drifting off in the night. ZZZzzzzzzz.

Name: MARRAM GRASS

Description: A green, grass-like plant with long leaves. Grows 50–120 cm tall.

Ideal site for planting: On the sloping sides of sand dunes

Planting tips: Don't bother about watering this bloomer. It's designed to cope with bone-dry conditions. For starters, its leaves are rolled up tightly so they don't leak loads of water into the air. And its tough, creeping roots are extra long for reaching water deep under the sand. It really gets to the root of the problem. But that's not all its rambling roots are good for. They're brilliant for binding the sand together and stopping the dune getting blown away by the wind. And if the marram grass gets swamped by sand, it simply sends out a load of brand-new shoots.

Name: CORD GRASS

Description: A bright-green type of grass with smooth, flat leaves. Grows about knee high.

Ideal site for planting: Salt marshes

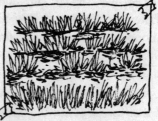

Planting tips: This bloomer's a real tough nut. Throw almost anything at it and it'll survive. It's perfect for planting in your salt marsh, where it's drenched in salty sea water twice a day. Salt can seriously harm a plant's health. But don't panic if the leaves look as if they're sprinkled with salty specks. Your plant's not about to drop dead. The specks are simply waste salt that the leaves have squeezed out.

Name: SEA LETTUCE

Description: A type of seaweed with crinkly, bright-green fronds. Looks a bit like, er, lettuce.

Ideal site for planting: In rock pools and around most coastlines

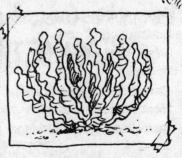

Planting tips: The great thing about this watery weed is that it can grow almost anywhere. So you can fix it on to rocks or leave it to float freely. And it doesn't even seem to mind if the water's not very clean. All in all, a really handy plant for plugging those annoying gaps. Apart from looking pretty, the sea lettuce's paper-thin leaves are yummy to eat, and packed full of vital vitamins. They're nibbled by sea snails, sea urchins, crabs and … hungry humans, who eat them raw in salads or deep-fried as a crispy snack. Go on – eat up your greens.

Horrible Health Warning

Forget going to the doctor. If you'd had tummy ache hundreds of years ago, your mum might have given you a spoonful of hairy hound's-tongue leaves boiled in wine. Don't worry. It's not like getting a wet, sloppy kiss from your pet pooch. Healing hound's-tongue is a seaside plant that grows on the slippery slopes of sand dunes. But you might have had to hold your nose. Oddly, hound's-tongue leaves pong like musty mice.

HMMM!

The Cracking Coasts Gardening Guide Presents
✿✿ BLOOM OF THE MONTH ✿✿

Our gardening experts are proud to present our plant of the month. It's far and away the pick of the bunch ... the marvellous, the mud-loving...

MANGROVE

Description: Check out the piccy below for a closer look...
Ideal site for planting: Along muddy, tropical coasts where rivers flow into the sea. (There's more about where to track down mangroves on page 30.)

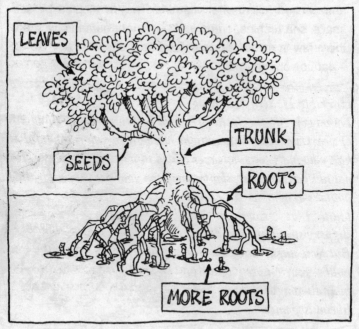

LEAVES

SEEDS

TRUNK

ROOTS

MORE ROOTS

Trunk: *Some mangroves are bush-sized, but others grow into huge trees up to 25 metres tall. So it depends how much space you've got.*

Roots: Plants need oxygen to breathe and there's not much of it in the mud that mangroves grow in. So they use some of their roots like snorkels. These sharp, spiky roots don't grow down into the ground. They poke up out of the mud and suck in air for the mangrove to breathe.

More roots: *Other roots sprout from the mangrove's trunk so it looks like the tree's walking on stilts. These sticky stilts sit like a raft on top of the gloopy, shifting mud and stop the tree slithering out to sea. Talk about being rooted to the spot!*

Leaves: Drying out is a problem for mangroves, and their thick waxy leaves stop loads of water being lost. Old leaves are also used for storing waste salt which could kill the tree. When the leaves fall off the tree, the salt's sent packing with them.

Seeds: *Mangroves have special seeds that sprout while they're stuck to a branch. Later, the seeds fall off the tree and float about for up to year before taking root in the mud. Then they bloom unusually fast before they're swept out to sea on the tide.*

What one green-fingered gardener said:

"They're the hardiest plants I've ever seen and a bargain to boot. I started off with a couple of trees and now I've got a whole bloomin' swamp. Besides, mangroves are marvellous for trapping mud and stopping your coastline being washed away. They also make lovely sheltered spots for baby fish, shrimp and prawn nurseries. Not a plant to be sniffed at."

Planting tips: You'll need to check your swamp regularly for mangrove worms. These pesky, slug-like creatures bore into the tree trunks and worm their way through the wood. (Actually, they're not worms at all but boring crustaceans.) If you can't get rid of them, try eating one or two. They taste like crab with a hint of wood. Apparently. Fancy a worm sandwich, anyone?

And you thought school dinners tasted revolting! So while you're busy picking bits of mangrove worm shell out of your teeth and stocking up on hound's-tongue to take the taste away, it's time to crack on into the next chapter. Forget surfing snails, clinging limpets and barmy barnacles. It's time for some horrible human company.

LIVING ON THE EDGE

It's official. The seaside's not simply a top spot for a holiday. It's also a cracking place to set up home. Don't believe me? Ask the three billion people (that's a staggering half of the world's population) who already live along the coast. Depending on your lifestyle, there's a mindboggling range of coasts to choose from. If it's peace and quiet you long for, try the chilly polar coasts of the Arctic or Antarctica. You might end up freezing to death, but at least you won't see another horrible human for months on end. If that's not your cup of tea, why not head for a bustling seaside city? There are plenty to pick from. But what on Earth is so great about living on the edge, apart from the stunning sea views? Time to pay a visit to the offices of Headland, Stump and Stack, estate agents right at the cutting edge.

Morning, sir or madam. Archie Headland, your friendly local estate agent, here. My firm has been specializing in seaside homes for years, you know. So if you're looking for your dream home, you've come to the right place. We've got hundreds of top-notch coastal properties to show you. And that's not all. Depending on where you'd like to live, you can choose from the following fabulous features.

Fancy a bit of ocean-fresh fish for your supper? Well, the coast's the place to live. For centuries, horrible humans have gone fishing by the sea. And no wonder. Fish are bursting with healthy proteins and vitamins, and you'll have buckets of them right on your doorstep. You can catch your fish the traditional way, using trusty old rods and lines, traps or spears. Or you can hire yourself a high-tech fishing boat. Where's the best place to get started? Head to the continental shelf. (That's just off the coast where the land slopes into the sea.)

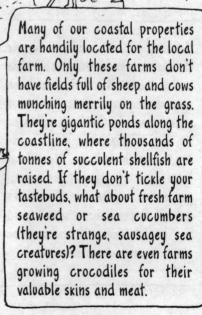

Many of our coastal properties are handily located for the local farm. Only these farms don't have fields full of sheep and cows munching merrily on the grass. They're gigantic ponds along the coastline, where thousands of tonnes of succulent shellfish are raised. If they don't tickle your tastebuds, what about fresh farm seaweed or sea cucumbers (they're strange, sausagey sea creatures)? There are even farms growing crocodiles for their valuable skins and meat.

Sign up for one of our homes today and you'll get a supply of genuine seaside sand for free. We've got billions of tonnes of the grainy stuff to give away. It's brilliant building work. But forget shovelling it up using buckets and spades. You'll need heavy-duty dredgers (monster sand-sucking machines) to shift this lot. We'll even throw in a sample of ground-up seashells (the ideal ingredient for making your cement set).

Fancy running your telly from the tides? Nope, it's not too far-fetched to be true. With all that water sloshing to and fro, there's masses of energy going to waste. And, because the tides happen twice a day, every day, results are guaranteed. With one of our do-it-yourself tidal power kits, you could soon be making enough ever-ready electricity to keep your home going for weeks. True, it's horribly costly but it's also shockingly easy to install.

What your kit includes:
• A barrage (that's the posh name for a monster dam with tunnels running through it)
• Some turbines (they're like giant wheels)
• Some generators (they're machines for making electricity)

What you have to do:
a) Find a river estuary and build your barrage across it.
b) Pop one turbine and one generator in each tunnel.
c) Now let the tide get to work. It'll flow in and out of the tunnels and turn the blades of the turbines. The turning turbines will drive the generators which make electricity.

And finally, pick the desperate Diamond Coast (a stretch of seaside desert in Namibia, Africa) to live on and you could find yourself the proud owner of a dazzling diamond or two. OK, so they'll cost you a fortune. After all, it's horribly hard work getting the diamonds out. First, machines have to dig up tonnes of scorching sand. Then the sand's sent to a processing plant where the diamonds are picked out. How on Earth did the diamonds end up in the desert? They were washed down to the coast by rivers millions of years ago.

Earth-shattering fact

If it's a genuine antique you're after, what about a fossil? Of course, you'll have to find a cracking cliff first. If it's made from the right sort of rock, you may find fossils hidden inside. Enterprising Mary Anning (1799–1847) turned to fossil-hunting to pay the bills when her dad died. (She later sold the fossils to tourists.) Luckily, she lived by the coast in Dorset, southern England, where the cliffs were chock full of fabulous fossil finds. Even so, chipping them from the rocks was risky work. Especially when the cliff started crumbling right beneath Mary's feet. But that didn't put fossil-mad Mary off. Among her most famous finds was the first-ever fossil of a plesiosaur, a kind of ancient, long-necked turtle. Until then, baffled boffins had no idea that this ancient animal had ever existed.

Could you be a honey hunter?

Long-lost fossils aren't the only horribly risky things to collect. Fancy some honey for tea? Count yourself lucky. You can just pop along to the shops and buy jarfuls of the stuff. Easy-peasy. But people who live in the swampy Sundarbans* don't have that luxury. First, they have to head into the forest to find a bees' nest. (Bet the bees are wild about that.) Reckon you've got what it takes to keep them company on their next hazardous hunting trip? It's a brilliant way to see the scenery … if you don't get stung or fall out of a tree. Here's what you'll have to do:

> * Head for the Sundarbans and you'll find yourself in the world's biggest mangrove swamp. It blooms around the enormous delta of the Ganges and Brahmaputra rivers in the Bay of Bengal (that's part of the Indian Ocean). And it's home to thousands of people who earn their living as fishermen, wood-cutters … and honey-hunters.

1 You'll have to wait until April or May to set off on your trip. That's when the forest flowers bloom so the bees can start making honey. Don't forget to join the honey-hunters in saying a special prayer to bless the hunt and keep you safe.

2 You set off by boat along the twisting channels criss-crossing the swamp. There are nine honey-hunters in your group including your leader. He's a hardened hunter who's especially skilled at spotting the best bees' nests.

3 You leave the boat behind and carry on by foot. The forest's in a terrible tangle here and the going's getting really tough. You soon find yourself knee-deep in mud and being eaten alive by mosquitoes. But ssshhh! Keep your voice down. You're entering tiger territory and tigers munch honey-hunters for lunch. Watch out for tracks and piles of droppings. They're sure signs there are tigers about. (Alternatively, try wearing a mask of a face on the back of your head. It'll trick the tigers into leaving you alone because they prefer to attack from behind. You hope.)

4 Just then, your leader spots a bees' nest high up in a forest tree. There's just one teeny problem. It's swarming with honeybees. You grab a bunch of tiger-fern leaves and set the leaves alight. Then you wave the flaming leaves all around the tree. The thick, black smoke should make the bees buzz off.

5 You wrap a scarf around your head and climb up the tree. Then you stick your hand into the nest to grab the gooey honeycomb. But you'll need to be quick. Despite the choking smoke (and your helpful headgear), chances are you'll still get stung. (If this happens, rub the stung bit of skin with herbal oil. It'll help ease the pain.)

6 You put the honeycomb in your basket and take it back to your village. Make sure you leave some comb behind in the tree so the bees can rebuild their nest. You eat some of the scrummy honey yourself and sell the rest at market.

Earth-shattering fact

Congratulations! You're back in one piece. (And the tiger teeth marks hardly show.) So how about a complete change of scene? For centuries, people have used the ocean for getting about. And the sea's still used today for moving people and goods. So where better to build a town or city than right by the coast? You'll have the sea on your doorstep so you won't have to go far for a lift. Some seaside settlements have grown into world-famous ports. (A port's a place by the sea or a river where ships pick up and unload their cargo.) Take

remarkable Rotterdam in Holland. It's the biggest and busiest port on Earth, handling a staggering 340 million tonnes of goods a year (mostly oil, chemicals, coal and iron ore). No wonder it takes 60,000 workers to keep the port up and running. Not bad for a place that started off as a paltry fishing village.

Extreme seaside sports

Fed up of lounging about in the sun? Looking to spice things up a bit? Look no further. Forget drippy dips in the sea. We've got some seriously exciting seaside sports lined up for you. But before you get into training, here's a word of warning. Some of the sports you're about to try are stomach-churningly dangerous. What's that? You've changed your mind? Talk about being a spoilsport. But you don't get off the hook that easily. While you're vegging out in your deck chair, you could always send Shelley to try them out instead.

Scary sport 1: COASTEERING

When they asked me to go and jump off a cliff, I said, "No way!" Well, would you? But here I am about to take the plunge. Ooohh! Better not look down. I'm not too good with heights. It's all part of a sport called coasteering. First, you put on a wetsuit and crash helmet (and a life-jacket, of course). Then you leap off the rocks into the sea. Next you swim through some really wild waves to the next craggy cliff ... where it all begins again. For an added thrill, you can go for a spin in a washing machine. That's the technical term for the surging swells of water around the bottom of the rocks. Right then, here I go...

Scary sport 2: KITE-SURFING

This sport sounds seriously scary but I'll give it a go. I think. I'm told it's a bit like windsurfing, only you've got a kite fixed to your surfboard instead of a sail. Then you let the wind whizz you through the waves. There's just one teeny snag – you'll be going horribly fast. But first you have to learn how to do something called body-dragging. And I'm dreading it, I can tell you. You don't bother with the surfboard. You just let the kite drag you at top speed across the sea. The only way to stop is to let go of the kite. On second thoughts, I'm outta here!

Scary sport 3: SAND-BOARDING

Sand-boarding's a bit like snow-boarding. You stand on a surfboard and hurtle downhill. Except this time you're surfing across sloping sand instead of slippery snow. So here I am, standing on top of a sand dune, ready to roll. I've picked quite a diddy dune to start with. It's not too steep so I won't go too fast. (And I won't have too far to walk back up for another go.) The trick's not to head straight down the slope but to sweep from side to side in long curves. Should be a cinch. And at least the sand looks nice and soft in case I fall off... Aagggghhhhh!

Scary sport 4: COASTAL SKYDIVING
I reckoned coastal skydiving sounded quite soothing. What a monster mistake! I'm 3,000 metres up in a plane, WAITING TO JUMP OUT!

[Seconds later] Help!!! I'm free-falling through the air so I can't chicken out now. Luckily, I'm strapped to an expert so I just hope they know what they're doing. Apparently, the view's brilliant and on a clear day you can see for miles. If you dare open your eyes.

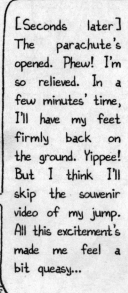

[Seconds later] The parachute's opened. Phew! I'm so relieved. In a few minutes' time, I'll have my feet firmly back on the ground. Yippee! But I think I'll skip the souvenir video of my jump. All this excitement's made me feel a bit queasy...

Teacher teaser

Is your teacher a cool surfer dude? Or a dreary old stick in the mud? Why not ask her this make-or-break question?

Which of these ISN'T a type of wave for a surfer to ride?
a) A beach break
b) A reef break
c) A tea break

Have you landed your teacher in the soup?*

Answer: c) A tea break's when your teacher puts her feet up and slurps down a cuppa or two. Nothing daring about that. But if she wanted to ride a) or b), she'd need to be a really chilled surfer. A beach break's a quite gentle wave that breaks on a sandy sea bed, so it's ideal for beginners. But a reef break's a much wilder wave that breaks over a coral reef. So you run the risk of a major wipe-out (that's a cool surfer term for falling off your board).

*By the way, soup's also surfer-speak for the frothy foam left behind after a wave has broken.

Wild weather warning

Living beside the seaside isn't all thrills and spills. Far from it. Sometimes seriously stormy weather batters the shoreline. Take hair-raising hurricanes (they're huge, spinning storms that form over warm, tropical seas), for starters. They whip up whopping waves that can flood low-lying coasts, causing devastating loss of life and destroying cities and towns.

But thundering hurricanes aren't the only coastal dangers. On 26 December 2004, a gigantic wave called a tsunami* struck coasts right around the Indian Ocean … WITHOUT ANY WARNING. By the time the wall of water had drained away, it left hundreds of thousands of people dead or homeless. Here's the terrible true story of that dreadful day…

*A tsunami (soo-nar-mee) is a series of massive waves usually triggered by deep-sea earthquakes, volcanoes and landslides. Tsunamis are sometimes wrongly called tidal waves. Even though they're nothing to do with tides.

Terrifying tsunami
26 December 2004

00.59 GMT* (07.59 local time) A colossal underwater earthquake strikes off the coast of Indonesia. The shaking lasts for eight earth-shattering minutes – a lifetime in earthquake terms. The quake rips apart the sea bed, forcing billions of tonnes of sea water upwards. This triggers a massive tsunami that races across the Indian Ocean faster than a jet plane.

*GMT stands for Greenwich Mean Time, the time used in Britain. In the countries hit by the tsunamis, the local times were all different. So GMT is used to make it easier to work out when events unfolded.

01.14 GMT The only people who know the quake's happened are scientists at the Pacific Tsunami Warning Center in Hawaii, thousands of kilometres away. According to their instruments, the quake measures a staggering 9.3 on the Richter Scale, making it the second most powerful earthquake since records began. But it's not the quake that's the real killer. And, at first, the scientists have no idea a tsunami's been unleashed. By the time they issue a warning, it's too late...

01.30 GMT Thirty minutes after the quake strikes, the first wave smashes into the Indonesian island of Sumatra. Out at sea, the tsunami's speedy but it's only about 30 cm high. But as it hits land, it slows down and rears up alarmingly until it's as tall as a three-storey building. People living along the coast see a sheer wall of water rising out of the sea. Wave after wave crashes ashore, sweeping away boats, cars, houses, shops … and people. A kilometre inland, the ferocious force of the water strips the trees from the mountain slopes. The isolated Andaman and Nicobar Islands are also devastated.

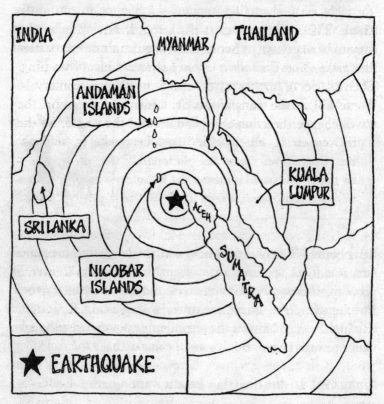

02.30 GMT Leaving Sumatra, the tsunami continues its trail of destruction and heads for southern Thailand. The beaches are crowded with holiday-makers enjoying a Christmas break in the sun. They can see the sea being sucked right away from the shore but they don't realize it's a warning sign. Many go down to the beach to collect shells and pick up stranded fish. Minutes later, the first wave hits, sending thousands of tonnes of water crashing down on them. Tragically, tourists and locals alike are trapped. Many drown in their homes or hotel rooms. Others are dragged out to sea.

03.00 GMT Racing west across the Indian Ocean, the tsunami strikes eastern Sri Lanka just a couple of hours after the quake. The first wave crashes ashore with no warning. Then a series of further waves hit at 5- to 40-minute intervals. Worse still, as the tsunami hits Sri Lanka's southern tip, the waves change direction and bend around the island. So the south-west coast, which should have been safe, is suddenly right in the path of the waves. With deadly power, the waves smash the shoreline to smithereens. Whole towns and villages are wiped out, not only in Sri Lanka but in south-east India.

04.30 GMT Next in line are the Maldives, one of the lowest-lying countries on Earth. These idyllic islands rise a meagre 4 metres above sea level. The waves flood the islands, leaving people clinging to palm trees to avoid being washed away. But the islanders count themselves lucky. The damage could be much worse. The islands' coral reefs help to protect them by stripping the waves of some of their energy.

07.00 GMT About six hours after the quake, the waves arrive on the east coast of Africa. Worst affected is Somalia, where fishing boats are engulfed by surging seas and hundreds of people are lost. And that's not all. The waves contaminate the drinking-water supply by poisoning it with salt. Kenya and Tanzania also feel the full force of the wave. But casualties are low. By now, most people have heeded the warning and moved to higher ground.

The tragedy unfolds...

In the days after the tsunami, the appalling scale of the disaster began to unfold. With tens of thousands of people dead, whole communities had been wiped off the map. And the death toll was rising all the time. Bewildered survivors searched frantically for their loved ones. But with communications cut across the region, information was hard to come by. Millions more people were left homeless. Many had lost everything – members of their families, homes, belongings and livelihoods. Clean water, food, shelter and medicines were needed urgently. Immediately, the countries affected were declared disaster zones and aid agencies such as the Red Cross began to send rescue teams. Around the world, people raised millions of pounds to help the tsunami's traumatized victims, many of whom were extremely poor. But for many people, especially in remote places, help was slow to arrive. They had lived through a nightmare and it will still take years to rebuild their shattered homes and lives.

Six facts about the Indian Ocean tsunami

• An estimated 2.3 million people were affected by the tsunami. Of the 225,000 casualties, 175,000 are thought to be dead. The rest are still missing. Millions more people were left homeless. But the exact number of victims may never be known.

• The following countries were all hit by the waves – Indonesia, Sri Lanka, India (including the Andaman and Nicobar Islands which are part of India), Thailand, the Maldives, Malaysia, Myanmar, Bangladesh, Somalia, Kenya, Tanzania and the Seychelles.

• Indonesia was the worst hit, especially the island of Sumatra. It lay closest to the centre of the earthquake and took the full force of the killer waves. More than 128,000 people died and 37,000 are missing. In just 15 minutes, the northern city of Banda Aceh was reduced to rubble and almost half of the people living along the coast (mostly poor farmers and fishermen) lost their livelihoods.

• In Sri Lanka, a crowded passenger train called the *Queen of the Sea* was struck by the tsunami as the water surged inland. More than 800 of the 1,500 passengers were drowned as the deadly water knocked the train sideways and sent the carriages cartwheeling into a ditch.

• Elephants helping to haul timber in the mountains of Thailand seemed to sense the wave coming. They began behaving oddly, stamping their feet, then breaking their chains and running away. It's thought that special bones in elephants' feet help them to pick up low rumblings coming from the Earth, long before humans can.

• After this devastating disaster, there are plans to build a tsunami warning system in the Indian Ocean, like the one in the Pacific. What happens is this. Pressure sensors on the sea bed detect a passing tsunami from the weight of the water. They send signals to a chain of buoys floating on the surface. The buoys pass the information on to a satellite, which sends it to a warning centre. Warnings can then be flashed out, telling people how long they've got to get out of the way of the wave. Sounds like a brilliant idea. Trouble is, this life-saving system's horribly expensive to install and many Indian Ocean countries are too poor to afford it.

An incredible story

Ari Afrizal from Aceh in Sumatra was helping some of his friends to build a house when the tsunami struck. Caught up in the wave, Ari was swept out to sea. Desperately, he grabbed a passing log and clung on grimly for the next 24 hours. Somehow he managed to make a makeshift raft from tree branches, roots and planks of wood. Every day, Ari waved at passing ships but none of them stopped to help him. For three days, he had nothing to eat or drink. Then he found some coconuts and drank their milk. At times, he almost gave up all hope of surviving his dreadful ordeal. Two weeks after the wave washed him away, Ari was finally spotted by a ship and rescued. "I had nearly given up all hope of living," he said, when he described his incredible story of surviving against the odds

COASTING ALONG

As well as living along cracking coasts, people have been exploring them for centuries. You might think "Why bother?" when you could stay at home and watch the telly instead. Well, that's OK for armchair explorers, but the intrepid travellers in this chapter couldn't sit still for long. They were desperate to get cracking. Some of them had goods to trade. They were in it for the dosh. Others were on the look out for new sailing routes. And some of them had simply been bitten by the exploring bug. But it wasn't all plain sailing for our plucky trailblazers. Not by a long chalk. Many explorers ended up on wild-goose chases. Or went and got horribly lost. And most of them diced with death. Fancy following in their footsteps? Yep, it's time to hit the rocky road. Time to meet some of the gutsy globetrotters who put cracking coasts well and truly on the map.

Hugging the coast

The seafaring Phoenicians (fen-ee-shuns) were superb sailors who lived along the shores of North Africa thousands of years ago. With no fancy maps or charts to guide them, they explored the Mediterranean Sea, sticking close to the coast in case they got lost. But they weren't just in it for the sightseeing. They

were out to make money by trading in gold, silver, copper, tin and wood (which they also used to make ships). And pretty soon, all this wheeling and dealing made the Phoenicians filthy rich.

But the Phoenicians' most-prized product was a purple dye made from slimy mucus from a kind of shellfish. They were even named after it. ("Phoenician" comes from an Ancient Greek word meaning "purple". Bet you were dyeing to know that.) People came from far and wide and paid a fortune for the sumptuous stuff. But only if they'd got pots and pots of dosh. According to ancient records, the dye was worth TWENTY TIMES its weight in gold. In fact, it was so colossally costly, only members of royalty could afford to dye their clothes with it.

Fancy having a go at making some dye of your own? (Be warned – it's a bit of a faff. But flog this little lot and you'll never have to save up your pocket money again.) Interested? Here's the (top secret) recipe:*

* By the way, these instructions were written by a long-dead Roman writer. So don't blame us if they don't actually work.

PURPLE DYE (TOP SECRET) RECIPE

What you need:
• Some murex (they're a kind of mollusc with long, spiny shells)
• A wicker basket on a rope
• Some bait (mussels will do nicely)
• Some salt
• A large lead pot
• Bucketloads of water
• A roaring fire
• A sheep's fleece (ready washed)

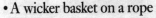

What you do:
1 First catch your shellfish. Pick a spot along the coast where the murex live among the rocks and corals. Then fill your basket with bait and chuck the basket into the water. (Don't let go of the rope.)

2 Wait for the murex to take the bait. Then haul your basket back up. You'll need to do this hundreds of times. It takes thousands of murex to make one diddy drop of dye.

3 Back home, squeeze each of the shellfish to get the slimy mucus out. (It's made in a special pouch in the murex's soft body.) But be warned, this could take you months.

4 Mix the mucus with loads of salt and leave it to soak for three days. This'll help to bring out the purple colour. Then boil it in the lead pot.

5 Next, add loads of water and simmer the mixture for another few days.

6 To test if the dye if ready, dip the fleece into the pot. Leave it for five hours or until it's a pretty shade of purple. (Don't worry about the fishy smell. It'll soon fade. Probably.)

Note: If you're squeamish about using shellfish, you could make a cheaper version of the dye instead. Use some draper's lichen (a lichen's a type of plant; a draper's a cloth maker) ground into a powder and mixed with water. Or try some dragon's blood (that's the purple gum from the trunk of a dragon tree. Nothing to do with dragons).

Horrible Health Warning
Even though the plucky Phoenicians were brilliant at it, exploring wasn't all plain sailing. Never mind fame and fortune. Some unfortunate explorers ended up suffering horribly – explorers like hardy English sea captain, Henry Hudson (1570–1611). In 1610, he set off on a daring voyage to search for a sea route across the top of North America. Things started off swimmingly. Hugging the north-east coast of Canada, Hudson stumbled on a brand-new bay, which he named after ... himself. After that, things went downhill fast.

His ship got stuck fast in the ice and the crew were forced to spend the freezing winter shivering on shore. When the ice began melting in spring, they wanted to head home. But hard-hearted Hudson refused to turn back. What did the crabby crew do? They shoved Hudson and his son into a small boat and set them adrift in the icy bay. Then they sailed off and left them to their freezing fate.

Around Australia

You might think that spotting a cracking coast would be simple. After all, they crop up all over the place. Especially if the coast you're looking for lies around awesome Australia. How on Earth could you miss that? But believe it or not, Australia was one of the last coasts to be explored. Why? Well, partly because it's so bloomin' big and partly because it's so bloomin' far away. Even getting to Australia meant a horribly long and risky journey. And to top it all, for centuries, no one knew if you could sail right the way round it. Yep, to be an Australian explorer you need to be an amazingly tough nut. And they don't come much tougher than the intrepid travellers that feature in this Horrible Geography Hall of Fame Special. Were they horribly brave? Or barking mad? You decide. And don't worry about getting horribly lost. Here's Shelley to show you around.

Horrible Geography: Australian Explorers' Hall of Fame

In 1642, salty sea-dog Abel Tasman set off for Australia to see if it was part of a mysterious Southern Continent. (This later turned out to be Antarctica, but no one knew that at the time because no one had actually been there.) If Abel managed to sail right round it, he'd prove it wasn't. If you get my drift. Trouble was, these were uncharted waters and no one knew what on Earth he would find. Abel set sail from Jakarta (in modern-day Indonesia) and headed east ... COMPLETELY MISSING Australia but discovering the islands of Tasmania and New Zealand instead. Two years later, he was back again. And this time he not only spotted Australia but also made a cracking map of its north coast. Bet he was ab-el to enjoy that trip. Ha, ha.

ABEL TASMAN
(1603 - 1659)
NATIONALITY: DUTCH

WILLIAM DAMPIER
(1651 - 1715)
NATIONALTY: BRITISH

When his mum and dad died, young William ran away to sea and joined the navy. Later, he ditched the navy and hitched a lift on a pirate ship. And he never looked back. He sailed as far as the USA, Hong Kong, Vietnam, the Philippines and even the Galapagos Islands. Talk about globe-trotting. In January 1699, daring Dampier was put in charge of an official expedition to explore the north-west Australian coast. (His pirate days were long gone by then.) Early in August, he landed in Shark Bay on the west coast. But he couldn't find any drinking water so he couldn't stay for long. After that, things went horribly wrong. On the way home, his ship sprang a leak and Dampier and his crew were stranded on Ascension Island in the middle of the Atlantic Ocean. Back in England, William wasn't the sort of person to settle down and put his feet up. He filled his time writing several best-selling books about his amazing adventures. What a guy!

JAMES COOK
(1728 - 1779)
NATIONALITY: BRITISH

Top British explorer James Cook was a brilliant sailor. (In fact, he was brilliant at everything except spelling.) So it's no surprise he was picked to lead some of the greatest expeditions in exploration history. In 1768, James set sail for the South Pacific on a daring new scientific voyage. At least, that's what he told everyone. Officially, James said he was heading for the island of Tahiti to monitor the movements of the planet Venus. But secretly, he had orders to search for the Southern Continent (remember it?), which still hadn't been found. Did Cook finally track it down? Nope, I'm afraid not. But he sailed along the coasts of Australia and New Zealand and filled in lots of the gaps on the maps. And he helped rewrite the geography books. How? Well, thanks to his daring journey, geographers now knew Australia was an island with cracking coast all the way round. My hero.

At the tender age of 15, Matthew joined the navy. (He'd been reading about Robinson Crusoe and fancied a life at sea.) Later, he sailed to Australia and explored bits of the coast in a titchy boat called "Tom Thumb". In 1801, Matt got married but his honeymoon didn't last long. He was soon off on his Australian travels again, leaving his wife at home. (They wrote loads of love letters to each other but they're much too sickeningly soppy to repeat here.) Matt's mission was to make a map of the whole Australian coast – a staggering feat. Amazingly, he pulled it off, but by that time his ship was so rotten he had to abandon it. Leaving him without a lift home. Matt soon hitched a lift on another ship but it ran aground on the Great Barrier Reef. Would it be third time lucky? Unfortunately not. Matt's next ship stopped at Mauritius (an island in the Indian Ocean), where he was arrested as a spy and thrown in prison for seven years. Finally, in 1810, Matt made it back to England to be reunited with his wife. But his rotten luck didn't really change. The book he wrote about his travels was published on 18 July 1814 ... the day, sob, before he died.

MATTHEW
FLINDERS
(1774-1814)
NATIONALITY:
BRITISH

The case of the lost lighthouse keepers

Being cast adrift or chucked in jail weren't the only horrible hazards facing our intrepid explorers. Sticking so close to the coast could be costly. Especially if you ran into rotten underwater rocks and your ship sprang a lethal leak. To stop this happening, many coasts boasted a lighthouse warning sailors to steer clear of the shore. Modern-day lighthouses have automatic lights, so it's dead easy to keep them glowing.

But in old-fashioned lighthouses, the keeper had to light the lamp by hand every day. This system usually worked brilliantly. Unless your lighthouse keepers went and vanished without trace. Sounds too spooky to be true? Well, that's exactly what happened on the wild island of Eilean Mor off the coast of Scotland. Here's the gripping true story...

Eilean Mor, the Flannan Islands, Scotland, December 1900

On the morning of 15 December 1900, a passing ship spotted something seriously wrong with the lighthouse on Eilean Mor. The light on the lighthouse had gone out. Or perhaps it had never been lit? Stranger still, over the next two weeks, nothing was heard of the three lighthouse keepers – James Ducat, Donald McArthur and Thomas Marshall. They seemed to have disappeared into thin air. And the mystery was set to deepen...

Unfortunately, bad weather stopped anyone reaching the island until 26 December, when the lighthouse relief boat was launched. On board was relief keeper James Moore.

"As we neared the island, we sounded the siren," he told the official enquiry that was later launched into the lighthouse keepers' whereabouts. "But there was no reply. The keepers usually come down to the jetty to help us land, but this time there was no one in sight. That's when I knew something must have gone horribly wrong."

Immediately, Moore jumped into the landing boat and rowed ashore. But the door to the lighthouse was shut and no one answered his frantic knocking. Moore unlocked the door and ran inside, calling out to the keepers. To his alarm, the place was deserted and the keepers were nowhere to be seen. And there were other ominous signs. The ashes in the fireplace were cold and the clock on the wall had stopped. The keepers' beds were empty and neatly made. Oddly, a meal lay half-eaten on the table.

"But there was no sign of the keepers," Moore continued. "They'd simply disappeared."

Moore rushed back to the boat and told the others what he had found. Then he went back to the lighthouse to make a more thorough search. Everything seemed to have been running smoothly. The last entry in the lighthouse records was 15 December – the day the light went out. But there was plenty of oil for the lamp and the lamp stood cleaned and ready for lighting.

"Something terrible must have happened, and happened suddenly to stop the keepers carrying out their duties," a tearful Moore told the enquiry. "I've known them since we were kids and they were the best keepers you could get."

During the official investigation, more details of that fateful day began to unfold. There had been a storm on the night of 14 December and the jetty showed signs of having been damaged. A box containing ropes and other equipment had also been washed away. It began to seem likely that the men had left the lighthouse to fasten this box down against the storm. The evidence quickly mounted up. The men were wearing wet-weather clothing and had locked the door behind them to stop it being blown open.

What on Earth had happened to the keepers after that? One suggestion was that they were blown off the edge of the rocks as they went about their work. But this could not have happened because the wind was blowing in the wrong direction that day. It seems more likely that the keepers were swept out to sea by an unexpectedly large wave. Rumours even started of a terrible row in which the keepers were killed. Whatever the keepers' final fate, this dreadful disaster was to haunt these isolated islands for years.

Modern-day exploration

Thanks to our explorers' exploits, brand-new charts (that's the posh name for sea maps) were made of miles and miles of the world's coasts. These cracking charts came in so handy that they were used for years and years. Trouble is, coasts are constantly changing (remember earth-shattering erosion?). So it can be terribly tricky keeping your charts up-to-date. Luckily, modern-day explorers have lots of mod cons to help them map coasts more quickly and precisely. Take satellites, for starters. They're used to take snaps of the coast from space. These space-age piccies can then be turned into amazingly accurate maps. But charts aren't just useful for finding your way from A to B. By showing up sunken rocks, sandbanks, and other ships, they also help to stop accidents happening at sea. And that's not all. They're what horrible geographers use to spot bits of crumbling coast and bits being poisoned by pollution. Pretty practical, eh?

Getting itchy feet? The good news is that there's lots of coast still left for you to explore. But you'll need to push the boat out. All over the world, cracking coasts are in a state of collapse...

CRUMBLING COASTS

Some coasts crumble away naturally over years and years, and you can blame earth-shattering erosion for that. But other coasts are under serious strain because of what horrible humans are doing to them. The trouble is, coasts are such popular places to live, work and go on holiday, that everyone wants to go there. I mean, would you rather spend a week by the seaside or being bored out of your skull indoors? And all these extra people are taking coasts right to the edge. So what on Earth are horrible humans doing to turn the coast to toast?

Seasick seashore

Feeling hot and bothered? Fancy a refreshing paddle in the sea? Sounds lovely, doesn't it?

PADDLE, NOT PIDDLE!

Well, you'd better watch out where you're putting your feet. Horrible humans are making the seashore sick by pumping sewage and dumping rubbish (like cans, bottles and even toilet paper) into the sea. Disgusting, eh? And we're not talking just slightly grubby. Some coasts are FILTHY. Still keen to dip your toes in? But hang on. Before you pop your socks off, here's a quick news flash...

CATASTROPHIC OIL SPILL THREATENS COAST OF DEATH

Disaster struck the rugged northern coast of Spain yesterday when the oil tanker *Prestige* split in two and sank in rough seas. The ship was carrying a cargo of 77,000 tonnes of deadly poisonous tar-like fuel oil. Enough oil to fill 250 Olympic-sized swimming pools has oozed on to the shore, making this one of the world's worst-ever oil spills.

The tanker began spilling oil a few days ago when it first ran into difficulties off the mainland. In an effort to stop the oil spreading, the authorities refused to let the ship come ashore. They hoped the oil would set solid in the deep, cold water and no longer keep leaking. But their plans were scuppered. The oil continued to leak at a rate of about 120,000 litres a day, forming an enormous slick. Now the split in the ship had sent thousands more tonnes of lethal oil washing ashore, spelling disaster for wildlife and for hundreds of kilometres of coastline.

Thanks to its clear water and sandy beaches, the coast is one of Spain's richest fishing grounds, world famous for its shellfish. But in the aftermath of this catastrophe, all fishing has been suspended and thousands of local fishermen face losing their livelihoods.

"We call it the Coast of Death because there are so many shipwrecks," one man told us, sadly. "But we never thought things would get this bad."

A clean-up campaign has already started. Some oil is being skimmed from the sea surface to stop the slick spreading. Then chemicals will be sprayed on the oil to break it into tiny globules. It is hoped these will then be carried out to sea. Meanwhile, thousands of volunteers are busy scrubbing and hosing oil from the rocks and cleaning oil-coated birds and animals. Over 15,000 seabirds have already been killed. (Oil clogs up birds' feathers so they can't keep warm and they die. It's also deadly poisonous if the birds eat it.) Some progress is being made but it's a mammoth task. Experts reckon it could take at least another ten years to mop up the mess. And no one knows how much oil might still be left inside the sunken tanker.

Saving the shore

For people living along the coast, pollution's only part of the problem. They're piling on the pressure by building beach-side homes and hotels too close to the edge of the cliffs. And the risk of floods is getting worse because of something scientists call global warming. Here's Shelley to give you the low-down.

What's happening is humans are pumping tonnes of poisonous gases like carbon dioxide into the atmosphere (from cars, factories and power stations). And these gases are stopping spare heat escaping, making the Earth horribly hot. Slowly but surely, the heat's melting the ice at the perishing poles ... sending sea level rising. To make matters worse, this global warming's heating up the oceans as well. And when seawater warms up, it expands (gets bigger) ... sending sea levels rising some more. So, in future, even a small-ish storm could set off some serious flooding.

So what on Earth are humans doing to stop the rot? Here are some of the steps you could take to protect your collapsing coast. But will any of them do any good? Or are they making matters worse? You'll have to make up your own mind. You could…

1 Build a seawall along the beach. For holding the sea back and saving your cliff. Curvy, wave-shaped walls work best. They break up the waves and make them much weaker. So erosion happens more slowly. You hope.

The upside: They're wonderfully long-lasting and they've been used along coasts for years and years.

The downside: They're horribly costly to build. They also get eaten away by the waves, making their bottoms a bit wobbly.

2 Add a line or two of groynes. Groynes are low, wooden fences built along the shore. Stick them in at right angles to the sea. They trap sand and pebbles and stop them being washed away by longshore drift (see page 62 if you can't remember what that is).

The upside: They help to build up the beach and soak up the force of the waves, slowing erosion down.

The downside: They get worn out quite quickly. And they stop sand and pebbles reaching other bits of the beach so it gets eroded instead.

3 Armour-plate the cliffs. Another way of stopping your cliff collapsing. But forget olde worlde knights on horsebacke. This armour's made from solid rock. Pile up loads of large boulders at the base of your cliff. Or use a stack of tetrapods instead. They're four-legged chunks of concrete. And nothing to do with dinosaurs.

The upside: They work like seawalls and break up the force of the waves. This slows down erosion so your cliff doesn't crumble so quickly.

The downside: The sea will shift your boulders so you'll need to keep replacing them. And tetrapods are a horribly ugly eyesore.

4 Stabilize your sand dunes. Sand dunes are horribly handy for flood control. The problem is when the sand shifts or blows away. So how do you get your sand dune to stay put? Take your pick of these sand-tastic suggestions:

a) Spray your dune with spray-on rubber. (It works like a giant plastic bag.)

b) Plant Christmas trees in it. (Their roots bind the sand together.)

c) Cover it with layers of twigs and branches. (They help more sand to pile up.)

The upside: Sand dunes look nice and natural. Especially if you plant them with some pretty, sand-loving grasses.

The downside: Strong winds, storms, rabbit holes and people trampling over them may still cause your dunes to collapse.

5 Shovel on some more sand. Beaches are brilliant buffers between the sea and your fragile cliff-face. But if your beach is still being washed away, try chucking on more sand. It's something lots of tourist resorts already do. They bring in lorry-loads of sand (dug up from the sea bed, old beaches or even bone-dry deserts) and dump it on the worn-out bits of beach.

The upside: You get to keep your sandy beach and it looks as good as new.

The downside: Trying to match the sort of sand you've got already can be tricky. You need to find stuff that's got the same size of sand grain and the same colour.

6 Do nothing at all. If none of the other options appeal, try leaving well alone. Seriously. Some experts now reckon it's much better to let nature take its course. And it's much cheaper than building a groyne or seawall.

The upside: Your cliff will crumble into shingle (small bits of rock) that'll soak up the power of the waves. And if your coast floods, turn it into a wildlife-friendly salt marsh.

The downside: You won't be able to stop your cliff crumbling or your coast getting flooded. But you could start twitching (that's birdwatching, not a nervous tic).

Horrible Health Warning

Another way of protecting your coast is with a murky mangrove swamp. But you'll need to grab one before they disappear. All over the world, mangroves are facing the chop. Over half of the world's mangroves have already gone for good. They're being cleared for firewood, timber and to make space for fish farms, rice fields and tourist resorts. And all of this is having a awful knock-on effect on the local people who rely on the shrinking swamps for their food and livelihoods. (Mangroves are ideal nurseries for baby fish and shellfish.) It's also putting their homes at risk. Mangroves make brilliant natural buffers against storms, hurricanes and tsunamis. And once they're gone, there's nothing to protect the coast ... or stop a full-blown flood.

IT'S ONLY A BIT OF FIREWOOD... WHAT HARM CAN IT DO?

A cracking future?

Sadly, your summer holiday is almost over and it's nearly time to pack up your bucket and spade. Never mind. You'll be back next year. Or will you? It all depends what the future holds for cracking coasts. Will seaside holidays soon be a thing of the past? Or are things not quite as gloomy as they sound? The good news is that people all over the world are trying to stop the coasts from crumbling and to clean up their act. They're working hard to find ways for people to keep on using coasts without damaging them too much. Is it working? Well, it's too early to give coasts the all clear yet. So there's still plenty of time for you to help out before you head off home. Try joining a quick beach sweep. All you have to do is head down to your local beach and help pick up any loathsome litter that people have left behind. But hold on just a tick. What's that odd-looking object sticking out of the sand? Is it an old bit of rubbish someone's chucked away? Oops! It's actually your hopping mad geography teacher you'd forgotten you'd buried up to his neck in the sand.

HORRIBLE INDEX